BURPEE AMERICAN GARDENING SERIES

ORNAMENTAL TREES

OCT   2003

BURPEE

AMERICAN GARDENING SERIES

ORNAMENTAL TREES

Charles O. Cresson

PRENTICE HALL GARDENING

New York ◆ *London* ◆ *Toronto* ◆ *Sydney* ◆ *Tokyo* ◆ *Singapore*

PRENTICE HALL GENERAL REFERENCE
15 Columbus Circle
New York, NY 10023

PRENTICE HALL and colophon are registered trademarks
of Simon & Schuster Inc.
BURPEE is a registered trademark of W. Atlee Burpee & Company

Library of Congress Cataloging-in-Publication Data

Cresson, Charles O.
    Ornamental trees / Charles O. Cresson.
       p.   cm.—(Burpee American gardening series)
    Includes index.
    ISBN 0-671-84646-9
    1. Ornamental trees.   I. Title.   II. Series.
  SB435.C82   1993
   635.9′77—dc20   92-6022
                                          CIP

Designed by Levavi & Levavi and Patricia Fabricant
Manufactured in the United States of America

First Edition
10 9 8 7 6 5 4 3 2 1

All photographs by Michael Dirr except as noted. Agricultural Research Service, USDA (pages 92–93); Charles Cresson (pages 44 bottom right, 50 upper left, 54 right, 59 bottom, 71 bottom, 72 top); W. Atlee Burpee & Co. (page 84).

Illustrations on pages 8, 9, 16, 22, 32, 34, 36 by Elayne Sears
Illustrations on pages 80–82 by Michael Gale
Horticultural editor: Suzanne Frutig Bales

In Appreciation

I wish to express my gratitude to those who helped me in the preparation of this book. First, I am greatly indebted to Chela Kleiber, whose eyes were the first to see the manuscript and who helped me to make innumerable improvements. I also wish to thank Rebecca Atwater and Rachel Simon, my editors at Prentice Hall, who were always there with encouragement, support, and assistance, no matter what. Jeff and Liz Ball have helped me in many ways, taught me how to write a book and generously provided invaluable technical support. My friends, the staff of the Scott Arboretum of Swarthmore College, particularly Jeff Jabco and Laurie Hinckle, made the job much easier; they and the library were always available to me, and the arboretum has been an exceptional education throughout my life.

   I am especially grateful to Suzanne Bales. Without her encouragement and faith in me, I would not have written this book.

   Finally, I would like to thank my family who gave me a love of trees and have shared in growing them, especially my brother, Richard, whose chain saw is always ready to make room for new ones.

Cover: Asiatic magnolias, shown here at Winterthur Gardens near Wilmington, DE., are among the most spectacular of early spring-flowering trees. The white star magnolias (Magnolia stellata), foreground, begin flowering slightly earlier than the pink saucer magnolia (Magnolia ×Soulangiana), background.

Preceding pages: Simplicity and grandeur: A mature grove of eastern white pine, Pinus Strobus.

CONTENTS

INTRODUCTION

One of the great satisfactions of life is to watch a young tree grow to majestic proportions as it reaches maturity. Results may not be long in coming, for many trees grow rapidly. This can be a lifelong fascination. Enlist the help of children when planting a tree and they will have an early start in this pursuit.

Trees are beautiful. Throughout the year, they give interest to the landscape. Tall, stately evergreen conifers provide fresh green color, even in the depths of winter, among the silhouettes of their deciduous counterparts. Spring foliage of some trees emerges in shades of red, purple, and even gold, and for a few trees, these colors will persist through the summer. People often think of a tree's beauty only in terms of foliage, but imagine the spring or summer spectacle of a large tree bedecked with flowers. Fall is the season of brilliant foliage, which can equal the brilliance of the brightest flowers. Colorful fruit and berries often last well into winter or even the following spring, catching the sun, contrasting with the snow, cheering dull days, and feeding wildlife. Some trees even transform the color of their twigs to reds, yellows and bright greens in winter as if seizing the opportunity to attract your attention and invite you outdoors for companionship.

Trees are the dominant element, the backbone, of most landscapes. They create the setting in which other plants grow. Established trees impart a sense of age and establishment even to young gardens in which other plants, such as shrubs and perennials, may still be quite small. Because it takes so many years to grow large trees, they should be preserved and cared for if you already have them.

Aside from their beauty and landscape value, trees have an additional, even greater importance: They help to preserve the environmental balance of our piece of the earth. They provide a habitat where wildlife can thrive. Trees clean the air, removing pollution and toxins while transforming carbon dioxide into oxygen. Their roots hold the soil, preventing erosion. Tree leaves make nutritious compost and mulch, which builds soil fertility and creates a home for organisms that become food for wildlife. Their flowers attract hummingbirds, and their fruit and seeds sustain numerous other birds through the winter. Their branches, especially evergreen branches, shelter birds in adverse weather. Even dead trees have a role in nature, because many animals and birds require their cavities for shelter and nesting.

Trees also contribute to our own comfort by preserving valuable resources. Deciduous trees provide shade and absorb heat in the summer, cooling your patio and house, and indeed the whole neighborhood. After leaf drop in winter, they allow the sun's rays to warm the earth. Evergreens on the windward side of your house will break the force of cold winter winds, reducing your heating bill. On a property containing several mature trees, routine care and trimming can provide wood for occasional use in the fireplace. Trees not only will save you money but, when well selected and placed in the landscape, can add to your property value.

Both shrubs and trees are long-lived, woody plants and may be so similar that the distinction is sometimes blurred. Generally, trees have single trunks and shrubs have many trunks, or woody stems. Trees are usually taller, although some small trees may be smaller than the largest shrubs. To confuse the matter even further, some large-growing shrubs can be trained as single-trunked small trees. Trees can also be multi-trunked. To keep it as simple as possible, the trees in this book are able to grow to more than 15 feet, and usually have just one trunk. Dwarf trees, including dwarf conifers, are not included.

Though not requiring a wet site, weeping willows grow and look best next to water. This golden weeping willow, Salix alba 'Tristis', is a special treat mirrored in the lake in autumn.

TYPES OF TREES

Trees vary tremendously. The most apparent difference is between deciduous and evergreen trees. Deciduous trees lose their leaves in winter. Evergreens hold their leaves all year 'round. In the North, most evergreens are needled conifers that bear their seeds in cones (pines and spruces, for example). Deciduous trees usually have broad leaves, and many, such as the maple, assume brilliant colors in autumn. Others, such as crabapples and fringe trees, delight us with a breathtaking display of flowers and perhaps colorful fruits. It must be pointed out, however, that not all evergreens are conifers and not all deciduous trees are broad leaved. In the South, there are many fine broad-leaved evergreen trees such as the southern magnolia (or bullbay) and the live oak. Larches, on the other hand, are deciduous conifers. In other words, although generalizations are helpful, there are exceptions.

Tree Forms and Shapes

Trees grow in a variety of shapes according to their kind. For example, conifers tend to be pyramidal and oaks are generally rounded. On the other hand, mutations of many trees have been discovered through the centuries that have shapes different from the norm. These mutations have been propagated specially for use in gardens. The columnar Lombardy poplar was a mutation found in Lombardy, Italy, nearly 300 years ago; it is now common worldwide. The weeping flowering cherry, also a mutation, was introduced from Japan.

Some tree shapes, such as espalier, are not natural. They are created by training and pruning, and without regular shaping will resume growing in their natural forms.

NATURAL TREE SHAPES

Vase shaped

Globe shaped

Weeping

Spreading

Pyramidal or conical

Fastigiate

ARTIFICIAL (MAN-MADE) SHAPES, CREATED BY TRAINING AND PRUNING

Pollarded   *Pleached*   *Bonsai*

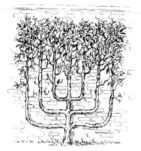
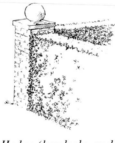

Espaliered   *Hedge (hemlocks and hollies)*

LEARNING ABOUT TREES

One of the best ways to learn about the trees that will grow well in your garden is to take a walk around your neighborhood and see what is growing nearby. Your neighbors probably have the same kind of soil and climate you do. Look at the kinds of locations and conditions where the healthiest trees are growing. Ask your friends about their trees; people usually enjoy sharing information about their gardens. Take a trip to a local public garden or arboretum where the names are often attached to the trees, so that you can find out what they are and learn more about them. Garden or arboretum staff members are often available to answer your questions. The cooperative or agricultural extension service in your state probably publishes free bulletins about trees. Reputable nurseries and garden centers also have knowledgeable staff that can answer your questions and recommend trees for local conditions. No book such as this can account for all climates and growing conditions, and the best advice will often come from those with experience in your area.

In the following pages you will learn the basics about trees: how to select them, how to grow them and how to solve their problems. The "plant portraits" will tell you about some of the best kinds for temperate climates.

THE GARDEN PLANNER

Before placing anything as permanent and important as a tree on your property, you should develop a scheme for how you will use and design the space. You probably already have ideas. Begin by looking at the different ways in which areas are used now. Look at how physical barriers such as hedges, fences and even your house and garage divide the property into sections. For instance, the front yard is probably separate from the back, but the side might be a separate area, too.

Next, consider what uses and activities are appropriate to various areas. The front area is likely to be viewed by the public. You want it to look attractive and inviting, but you may not spend much time there. The back is more likely to be private, and reserved for family activities and recreation. It may include a patio or deck for outdoor living. Consider the layout of your house, as well as your yard. Walk around inside your house and look out the windows. Think about the views from important rooms, such as your living room and den. You will need a utility area where trash cans, firewood and compost can be kept out of sight. You might want a flower garden, located in either sun or shade, and a vegetable garden, which will need to be in sun. All of these considerations will help you make your whole garden more attractive and functional. Placement of trees will be one of your first decisions in shaping these areas. (Chapter 2 explains what kinds of trees to plant for various purposes in your garden.)

YOUR GARDEN'S ENVIRONMENT

Now consider the characteristics of your piece of land. Look at the USDA Plant Hardiness Map of the United States (pages 92–93) to determine your approximate climatic zone. This map is based on normal winter cold, the most important factor in determining winter hardiness of plants. Local conditions also influence your climate. If you live at a high elevation, your climate will be colder than an elevation several hundred or thousand feet lower. A south-facing slope will be hotter and drier than a north-facing one because its angle catches more of the sun's rays. This means that if you have a south slope or a lower elevation you may be able to grow a plant that is not hardy for other properties nearby, even if they're in the same USDA hardiness zone.

The weeping Alaska cedar, Chamaecyparis nootkatensis *'Pendula', is a particularly graceful conifer.*

Rainfall

Find out the average annual rainfall for your area, and during which seasons it falls. This is not as critical as the characteristic temperature extremes, because you can water to supplement shortages of rain. Most trees need about 40 inches of rain per year to grow well, so in climates with little summer rain, you will need to water many trees. Some kinds will get along with less water, so if you live in a dry region it is especially important to get advice on what these trees are to avoid the need for extra watering.

Soil

Soil is an important feature of your garden's environment. Water availability is related to soil conditions. Sandy soils dry out quickly because the water drains right through. Clay soils hold water but are heavy and difficult to work; they are often compacted, with poor aeration and poor drainage. Roots need oxygen to grow, so they need good aeration in the soil. If puddles take more than half a day to seep in after a rain, you can tell your soil has poor drainage.

Drainage is also affected by topography. On a slope, the uppermost soil is likely to be dry, whereas the lower part will stay moist longer. Fortunately, many desirable trees thrive in adverse soil conditions, whether the soil be poorly drained or very dry. And don't despair; soils are usually mixtures of sand, clay and other particles that combine the advantages of each and are suitable for most of the trees you would wish to plant.

One condition few plants can tolerate is severe root competition. Densely matted, shallow roots take all the nutrients and water before less-established plants have a chance at them. Norway maples are notorious for their tenacious roots. If you have one, you'll note few things will ever grow beneath it. Some people have tried adding a layer of soil over the roots, but that is eventually a harmful measure: Generally it leads to the slow death by suffocation of venerable specimens. The roots are still there and will grow up into the new soil, if the tree survives. Filling over tree roots with additional soil changes the delicate balance of aeration to the roots.

Soil pH is one of the most important indicators of the suitability of your soil for specific plants; pH is a measure of the acidity or alkalinity of the soil, a scale that runs from 0 to 14. Below 7 is acid, and above 7 is basic (or alkaline). Rhododendron and their relatives, such as sorrel trees, are well known for requiring acidic soils. Soil pH affects the availability of many nutrients, and an extreme pH can actually cause a nutrient deficiency even though there is plenty of the nutrient in the soil. The best balance of available nutrients for most plants occurs near neutral, specifically pH 6.8. Most trees prefer slightly acidic soils, but many will grow satisfactorily in slightly alkaline soils, too.

The best way to learn about your soil is to have a soil test done. You can often buy a special envelope from the cooperative extension service of your state or from a local garden center, fill it according to directions, and send it through the mail to be tested by professionals. The results will tell you the pH, nutrient availability, and how to correct your soil in order to grow what you would like. The cost is generally modest, and a real bargain considering the invaluable information it furnishes about your soil.

Sargent's cherry, Prunus Sargentii, *is one of the finest flowering trees for early spring, but the early flowers are often spoiled by frost. In this situation, the pond may save the flowers by radiating enough heat to prevent light frosts.*

Air Circulation

Winds can hamper good tree growth. Surrounding trees, buildings and hills provide shelter from the wind. Hilltops and coastal locations are especially windy. Very sheltered sites, on the other hand, may have such poor air circulation that they encourage disease for susceptible trees, particularly in humid climates.

Sunlight

The amount of sunlight you receive determines the kinds of trees you can grow, too. Large surrounding buildings or trees on the south side cast a lot of shade, but the same trees on the north side will cast little shade. Overhead trees can cause heavy or light shade, depending on their size, type and how they are trimmed. Such densely foliaged trees as Norway maples cast a heavy shade, whereas oaks allow dappled sun to shine through. High shade is brighter and can be created by removing lower limbs along the trunk. Many trees and other plants can be grown well in high or dappled shade.

Existing Trees

If you already have trees on your property, your first priority should be to incorporate them into the landscape plan. Before removing any tree, be sure it really must go. A tree hastily removed and later regretted will take decades to replace. Of course, there are situations in which a tree cannot stay. It may be simply dead or damaged or sick beyond recovery. Perhaps it is just in the wrong place and you can't plan around it.

If you are considering removing a tree, first try to work with it. Ugly or misshapen trees can become fascinating specimens with great character. Through imaginative pruning you can reveal interesting trunk character, branch shapes and bark texture. You will create effects that can't be purchased at any price and that take years to develop. A low-branched tree that seems to be in the way can be limbed up, leaving an overhead canopy. If trees are too crowded, thin out the stand by selecting the best specimens in the best locations and removing the rest. Don't be overzealous—you can always take out more later. These decisions can affect the success of your property's design, and mistakes can take years to fix. If you feel unsure, seek the help of an experienced horticulturist or arborist with some design background.

DESIGNING WITH TREES

THE CHARACTER OF TREES

Because of their size, trees are dominant elements in any landscape. By virtue of their grandeur, they set scale. Alone or combined with shrubs, they shape your landscape and garden by enclosing it or dividing it into sections for different uses. They can create vistas and channel the eye toward desired points or block out and hide unsightly objects or areas. Overhead, they break the force of the sun to make a restful patch of shade. In addition, the trees you choose will shape the character of your garden.

Manipulate the sense of scale to your advantage. A very large tree next to a small house will dwarf it, whereas a large tree next to a large house will make it seem less imposing. Large foliage, like that of some magnolias, tends to make a small space such as a courtyard seem even smaller. In the landscape, large or coarse foliage will appear to be closer. The fine foliage of needled evergreens, such as spruce, recedes in the landscape, giving a greater sense of distance, losing detail and focusing attention on the overall tree shape.

Tree forms and shapes are as important as scale. Upright trees draw the eye up. Weeping trees draw the eye down. Pyramidal shapes attract attention to that part of the landscape and can add to the formality or symmetry of a design. They attract attention most dramatically when used singly or in pairs. High-branched trees allow us to see past the trunk, to focus on a distant object; they have space and air under them. Low-branched trees present a visual barrier in the landscape and stop the eye. They seem anchored to the ground and act as dividers. See pages 8–9 for illustrations of tree shapes.

The type of foliage plays a role in the character of design. Dark evergreen foliage can be somber, even overpowering; but used in moderation, or mixed with other foliage, it can create an attractive contrast or background to lighter elements that change with the seasons. For instance, bright yellow witch hazel flowers will show up more effectively in midwinter against a dark background of evergreens. Colorful crabapple fruits are particularly visible after their leaves have fallen, and even more so when they are backed by an evergreen. Foliage of deciduous trees and shrubs is usually of lighter shades of green. Deciduous trees are welcome additions to the winter garden, because after their foliage has fallen, more light reaches into dark corners on dull days. Illustrations of leaf shapes are found on the following page.

A classic combination of flowering dogwood, (Cornus florida) and azaleas.

LEAF SHAPES

Foliage type and shape varies widely from one tree species to another. Understanding basic foliage shapes is critical to identifying and choosing the right tree for landscape use. "Plant Portraits" describe basic leaf types as shown below.

BROAD-LEAVED SHAPES:

Simple

Palmately lobed

Pinnately lobed

Trifoliate

Palmately compound

Pinnately compound

Bipinnately compound

NEEDLED SHAPES:

Scalelike needled (i.e., arborvitae)

Short needled (i.e., spruce)

Long needled (in clusters, i.e., pine)

The magnificent autumn color of this deciduous conifer from China, Pseudolarix Kaempferi, *inspired the common name of golden larch*.

The native red maple, Acer rubrum, *is so named for its brilliant autumn color. It grows best in sunny locations. Here it grows with poplar, a pioneer species, that has not yet assumed its autumn color.*

Dwarf Trees

There are many kinds of dwarf trees. Some, such as Japanese bonsai, are kept small by pruning the shoots and roots regularly so that they are not allowed to grow large. But most dwarf trees in gardens are either genetically small or are dwarfed by being grafted onto dwarfing rootstocks. Genetic dwarfs naturally grow more slowly. In time they may become quite large, but it will take many years and they will never reach the size of their normal counterparts. Examples of genetic dwarfs are many varieties of conifers, smaller-growing forms of Japanese maples and some kinds of fruit trees, such as the small peach trees bred for patio containers.

Other trees, primarily apples and pears, are grafted onto roots developed by breeders to stunt the tree's growth. The relationship between the top of the tree and the different root is complex, but it is known that certain rootstocks will grow a tree of a very specific height and vigor. Dwarf fruit trees are most useful to growers or home gardeners who wish to pick fruit without the need of a ladder. Dwarfing rootstocks are less frequently used for ornamental trees.

SEXUALITY AND TREES

Although the great majority of trees are hermaphroditic (possessing both sexes on the same tree), there are a few, such as hollies, that are dioecious (having male and female flowers on separate trees). Male trees do not bear fruit, and neither will females unless there is a male tree nearby to provide pollen. Because hollies are grown for their attractive red berries, it is essential to have both sexes in your garden or neighborhood, along with a population of bees.

Luckily, bees frequent most gardens and can effectively pollinate about eight female trees from a single male tree. Bees are such efficient pollinators that the trees don't even have to be planted next to each other. Bees find all the trees, and travel freely between them. Many gardeners plant a male tree in a less prominent location and put the females where their berries will be most visible. Most nurseries stock both male and female cultivars of dioecious species, so you will be able to buy both sexes in order to have berries.

YOUR GARDEN

Trees help define and enhance garden areas. They are such dominant elements that they should be the first plants you place, if possible. Shrubs, perennials, annuals and bulbs should follow, in that order. The remainder of this chapter will explain how to fit trees into the landscape and what to look for in trees you are selecting for different uses.

Design Principles

Several design principles will assist you in evaluating the success of your garden and the fea-sibility of your ideas. Repetition of plants, objects, colors and forms help to unify a landscape. For example, you might place a tree in the foreground, and then place another one or more of the same kind in the distance. The eye will be drawn through the landscape as it moves from one tree to the next. In a small garden it may not be possible to repeat such large elements as trees, particularly when you want several different kinds to provide interest at different seasons. Instead, consider repeating smaller elements such as shrubs and choose kinds that will complement trees by blooming at the same time. (You can figure this out by observing your neighborhood or visiting public gardens.) You could also repeat a shape with smaller-growing trees of a different kind, but with a similar appearance.

Balance, or equalizing weights visually in the landscape, also imparts unity to a design. For instance, in a formal design, symmetry will provide balance, perhaps in the form of two identical trees on opposite sides of an object or space. It is slightly more complicated to achieve a sense of balance in an informal, asymmetrical scheme. But again, the concept of balancing visual weights applies. Create balance by using a large object on one side and several smaller ones on the opposite side. You can also use a large object closer to the pivotal point on one side to balance a smaller object placed farther away on the opposite side.

A focal point helps to unify a design by encouraging the eye to focus on a particular object or element, whether the setting be formal or informal. This simply means that a single element or area should stand out, and the design should be balanced on either side of it. The focal point may be a tree, shrub or flowers, but a nonplant feature, such as a bench or statue, is likely to be most effective because, being different, it will stand out better.

The principle of sequence uses time to create a progression of such seasonal features as bloom of different plants, foliage colors and winter interest. The greater the variety of plants

Few flowers can match the winter beauty of hollies with evergreen foliage and red berries. The variegated leaves of this English holly, Ilex Aquifolium 'Golden King', are an extra feature.

in your garden, the greater the potential for a continuous sequence of events and display. But the need for variety must not undercut repetition and balance, which are so necessary to good design. The principle of sequence itself should be used according to the principles of repetition and balance. All the seasonal interest should not be confined to one spot, but be repeated and balanced throughout the garden.

Think in terms of plant combinations. Combine trees and other plants to bloom together with complementary colors. Flowering dogwood with azaleas is a classic spring combination in many regions. Harmonious foliage color and shape provide a long season of interest. A single golden-foliaged Hinoki false cypress is a striking exclamation point among Colorado blue spruces and deep-green Norway spruces. Plant larger-leaved deciduous trees with needled conifers, for a contrast of textures. Locate an early pink-flowering saucer magnolia in front of a background of dark evergreens.

Needless to say, planting a small tree that will become a large specimen someday requires long-term vision. Full size may come in about 30 years for a flowering cherry, 50 to 60 years for a pin oak, or several hundred to a thousand years for a giant redwood. How should a gardener deal with the continuously increasing size of a tree when designing a planting? Landscape architects decide on a target time at which they want a landscape to "mature." This might be 5, 10 or more years.

Middleton Place, near Charleston, S.C., is famous for its old, magnificent, spreading live oaks, Quercus virginiana.

Oriental spruce, Picea orientalis, *is one of the best garden spruces because of its refined shape.*

This is the time at which the trees reach the size for which they were spaced. Of course, you can't stop them from growing, so after that the landscape may become crowded and need some major revisions.

In a commercial landscape, the plan may be to remove half the trees in 10 years when they become crowded. For the homeowner this is usually not a happy prospect. We become attached to our trees. Besides, they are a major investment in time and, perhaps, money. In home gar-

dens, it is usually best to place trees to allow for their mature size, especially large-growing, long-lived kinds such as oaks, tulip trees and pines. Mature spread must be considered, as well as mature height. Use smaller, shorter-lived cherries, dogwood and mountain ashes to fill in the spaces. They will have finished their life cycles by the time the larger trees finally mature. Face down and fill in the planting with shrubs and perennials.

CHOOSING TREES FOR SPECIAL PLACES

About Shade Trees

All too often shaded areas have a barren appearance because there is not enough light for most flowering and foliage plants to grow well. A more hidden problem is competition in the soil from shallow tree roots. This need not be. The best shade trees are those that have deep roots and branch from high on the trunk. Deeply rooted trees are compatible with shade plants and will allow you to create an attractive garden in the shade. Such shallow-rooted trees as lindens and Norway maples cause severe competition with underplantings for water and nutrients.

High shade is preferable to low shade because it allows more diffused light from the side for plantings beneath, yet it still breaks the force and heat of the overhead sun. High shade also allows more air circulation, which contributes to plant health, as well as human comfort on hot days. Another issue to consider when assessing the quality of shade is the density of foliage. It's easier to grow plants in the light shade of a honey locust than the heavy shade of a densely foliaged linden.

Broad-leaved trees make the best shade trees because of their spreading habits. Most are deciduous, but in the South, such evergreens as live oak are widely used. Conifers are less suitable as shade trees because they tend to be narrower. But if you have a grove of mature conifers, don't cut them down! They can be adapted to provide the right kind of shade by such techniques as limbing up (removing lower branches) and by thinning them out—removing the more crowded, weaker individuals.

Evergreen and deciduous trees cast different kinds of shade and have different uses on your property. Although evergreens impart a refreshing green to the winter landscape, too many of them will cast a somber darkness on those short, dull days. Evergreen trees provide more shelter to plants growing under them, especially evergreen shrubs, because they block the

---

Some Shade Plants for Under Trees

SHRUBS:

Camellia species
Enkianthus campanulatus
Hamamelis species (witch
  hazel)
Hydrangea species
Pieris japonica (Japanese
  andromeda)
Prunus Laurocerasus
  (cherry laurel)
Rhododendron species
  (includes azaleas)
Viburnum species

PERENNIALS:

Anemone × *hybrida*
  (Japanese anemone)
Astilbe species
  (goatsbeard)
Cimicifuga species
  (bugbane)
Dicentra species (bleed-
  ing heart)
Epimedium species
  (barrenwort)
Hosta species (plantain
  lily)
Pulmonaria species
  (lungwort)

GROUNDCOVERS:

Euonymus Fortunei
  (wintercreeper,
  euonymus)
Ferns, various
Hedera Helix (English ivy)
Liriope species (lilyturf)
Pachysandra terminalis
  (Japanese spurge)

BULBS:

Caladium species
Colchicum species
Crocus species
Narcissus species
  (daffodil)
Scilla sibirica (Siberian
  squill)

ANNUALS:

Begonia species
Browallia americana
  (bush violet)
Coleus species (flame
  nettle)
Impatiens species (busy
  lizzy)
Torenia Fournieri (wish-
  bone flower)

Weeping willowleaf pear, Pyrus salicifolia *'Pendula', is prized for its silvery foliage and pendulous mounded habit.*

winter sun and wind, which can cause winter burn. On the windward side of a building they break chilly winds, saving on heating bills. But don't use them on the sunny side; they will block the sun's warmth. Use deciduous trees on the sunny side where they will shade the house from the hot summer sun but allow the sun to provide some heat in winter. A deciduous tree on the south side of a patio will make it a sunny, warm and more inviting place in early spring, as well as a cool shaded spot through the summer. In the garden, spring flowers prefer to be planted under deciduous trees. Daffodils, crocuses, winter aconites and many other early bulbs begin growth in late winter when the bare trees allow plenty of sun to shine through. By the time trees leaf out, the bulbs will have nearly finished growing.

SCREENING TREES AND WINDBREAKS

Some trees can fulfill these three functions: visually hiding an unwanted view or object, absorbing or reducing noise, and breaking the force of strong winds. They should be well branched to the ground, and evergreen to function fully through the winter. Deciduous trees are usually not as effective in winter, but when wider plantings, such as a strip of woods, can be made on larger properties, they can function equally well. On small properties, evergreens with a narrow habit are preferable to save space. In very tight spaces, hedges are the only option. Large hedges are a lot of work to trim but can be successfully made from hemlock (*Tsuga canadensis*), white pine (*Pinus Strobus*), arborvitae (*Thuja occidentalis*) and holly (*Ilex* species). Small hedges should be made of shrubs.

Good planning is essential to the long-term success of a screen planting. The results of impulsive planting can be unfortunate and far-reaching. Planting a single row of large-growing conifers in too much shade or too little space can mean that in a few years the trees will have lost their low branches, with the screening effect lost and the trees casting too much shade to permit another effective screen to be planted beneath them. If space is at a premium, consider such small shade-tolerant evergreen trees as hollies or arborvitaes (*Thuja occidentalis*) or use shrubs.

Eastern arborvitae, Thuja occidentalis, *is an evergreen well suited to tall hedges and tolerates some shade.*

European hornbeam, Carpinus Betulus *'Fastigiata', makes a fine deciduous hedge, as seen here at Longwood Gardens, Kennet Square, Pa.*

Recommended Trees for Hedges

Carpinus Betulus 'Fastigiata' (European hornbeam)

Chamaecyparis pisifera (Sawara false cypress)

× *Cupressocyparis Leylandii* (Leyland cypress)

Fagus sylvatica (European beech)

Ilex species (holly)

Juniperus species (juniper)

Pinus Strobus (eastern white pine)

Prunus lusitanica (Portugese cherry laurel)

Quercus ilex (holm or holly oak)

Thuja occidentalis (eastern arborvitae)

Tsuga canadensis (hemlock)

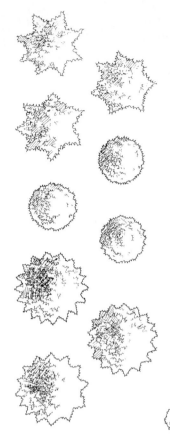

Left: To make a staggered tree planting more interesting, group several different kinds of trees. Plant trees that will be smallest when full grown in front. If you plan to plant three small trees, place two of them toward the front.

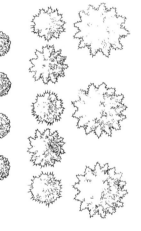

Right: Shrubs can fill in the "spaces" in a staggered row of conifers. Avoid large shrubs, and don't plant them so close as to crowd the tree, as they can shade the trees' lower branches.

Proper spacing is important to allow for the long-term growth of trees. If planted too closely and not trimmed, the stronger trees will gradually crowd out the weaker ones in an irregular pattern. Alternatively, when young trees are given enough space to grow, it will be many years before they fill in the gaps. The best solution is to space the trees widely in two staggered rows. When viewed straight on, the trees in one row will appear to fill the spaces between the trees in the other row. To fill the spaces even faster, interplant with shrubs. A less monotonous scheme is to use several groups of different kinds of trees.

Vegetation windbreaks are superior to the solid barriers produced by fences, walls and buildings, for several reasons. Because they allow air to pass through, they break the force of the wind without channeling it around the edges. (Wind can whip around solid objects, increasing in velocity and the potential to cause damage. Anyone living in a city in the midst of tall buildings knows this phenomenon well.) A windbreak of moderate density can reduce wind speeds for a distance of up to eight times its height. In addition, the permeability of vegetation windbreaks increases the area of the quiet zone behind the windbreak.

The effectiveness of sound reduction is enhanced by the density of foliage closest to the ground and by distance. The density of low foliage is most important because sound, such as road noise, travels along the ground. A sound barrier is most effective when planted close to the source of the noise, with as much distance as possible between the barrier and the listener. The initial volume of the sound is broken by the barrier, and then the remaining volume decreases while traveling the distance to the listener.

Screen plantings are valuable long-term investments. Protect them from crowding by any weed trees, shrubs and vines that might grow up with time; these create shade that will cause the foliage to thin out, and branches, especially low ones, to die out. If you give screen plantings enough space and keep them free from competing vegetation, they require little maintenance.

ABOUT SPECIMEN TREES

A tree considered a specimen or focal point is in a prominent location and has striking features, flowers or unique foliage color, for example. For the best effect, it must not be crowded. A specimen tree should be chosen with care, so that its mature size will be in proportion to the property. A small tree is often the best choice for a home garden of moderate size. It stands to reason that a prominently placed tree should possess as many striking features as possible, whether they be flowers, fruit, foliage or overall form. Crabapples (*Malus* species) and mountain ashes (*Sorbus* species) have both flowers and decorative fruit, but one must take care to select disease-resistant varieties that will not defoliate at the height of summer. Golden-rain tree (*Koelreuteria paniculata*) has yellow flowers in summer, strikingly coarse, deep green foliage and papery pods that hang into the winter. Weeping English beech (*Fagus sylvatica* 'Pendula') lacks showy flowers or fruit, but its magnificent pendant form is sufficiently striking when provided with enough space in a large landscape.

TREES FOR WILDLIFE

Consider wildlife when selecting trees for your garden. Birds and other animals add beauty and interest to the landscape during all seasons. To encourage these creatures to stay in your garden, you will want to plant a variety of trees, to provide them with fruits and seeds over a long period of time. Some fruits become palatable earlier than others. Less tasty types will be left alone until later, when the more favored kinds are no longer available. Robins and cardinals like the fruit of dogwood (*Cornus* species), crabapples (*Malus* species), mountain ashes (*Sorbus* species), hawthorns (*Crataegus* species), hollies (*Ilex* species) and junipers (*Juniperus* species). Seeds of birches (*Betula* species), sweet gums (*Liquidambar* species), spruces (*Picea* specics) and pines (*Pinus* species) are eaten by goldfinches. In autumn, squirrels bury acorns and other nuts to provide food all winter long. Hummingbirds are attracted to the flowers of many trees, including horse chestnuts (*Aesculus* species) and black locusts (*Robinia* species). Many birds feed on the insects that live on trees among the foliage, branches and bark crevices.

Trees provide safe places for nesting and shelter from inclement weather. Evergreeens are especially valuable for shelter in winter. Cavities in dead trees and branches are required by many species of birds and animals for nesting, but because few dead trees are left standing in residential areas, birdhouses hung on living trees are good substitutes. Each species has its own preference as to the type of house and tree. The greater the variety of trees and other plants, the better wildlife habitat you will have.

Junipers have soft, berry-like cones. Many ripen to a bluish color, as in the case of western red cedar, Juniperus scopulorum, *and are eaten by birds.*

Some Trees Adapted to City Conditions

MODERATE SIZE	NORMAL LANDSCAPE SIZE
Acer campestre (hedge maple)	25 to 35 feet
Crataegus species (hawthorn)	15 to 30 feet
Koelreuteria paniculata (goldenrain tree)	30 to 40 feet
Malus species (crabapple)	12 to 20 feet
Pyrus Calleryana (callery pear)	20 to 40 feet
LARGE SIZE	
Betula nigra 'Heritage' (river birch)	40 to 70 feet
Cercidiphyllum japonicum (katsura tree)	40 to 50 feet
Fraxinus species (ash)	50 to 80 feet
Ginkgo biloba (maidenhair tree)	60 to 80 feet
Sophora japonica (Japanese pagoda tree)	50 to 70 feet
Zelkova serrata (Japanese zelkova)	60 to 80 feet

ABOUT STREET AND CITY TREES

Conditions in the city present special challenges to trees. City soils are often compacted by machinery and foot traffic and surrounded by pavement. These conditions result in poor soil aeration. City trees are also constantly assaulted by air pollution. When the wrong trees are chosen for street planting, they can grow too large for the space available. Their tops threaten utility lines and may be cut off, resulting in the kind of open wounds where the exposed stubs are most susceptible to decay-causing fungi. Their roots heave pavement, sidewalks and curbs out of line. Nevertheless, street trees need to be large enough to form a trunk with the lowest branch about 8 feet high for

Callery pears, Pyrus Calleryana, *make fine street trees.*

pedestrian and small vehicle clearance. On the street side, low branches should be 14 feet high to allow for big trucks.

Fortunately, most of these problems can be averted by selecting trees of moderate size. For locations away from the street,

where more space is available, it is still important to select trees tolerant of pollution and soil compaction.

SEASONAL FEATURES OF TREES

Trees are year-'round companions in our gardens. They change their appearance; but unlike herbaceous plants, which die down, they remain standing, even after their leaves have fallen. We often think of trees as large foliage plants, but many have a season of prolific bloom or showy fruit.

The greatest number of trees flower in spring. Who could deny the breathtaking beauty of a saucer magnolia in full bloom, covered with pink petals in advance of its summer foliage, or the graceful Japanese flowering cherries in our nation's capital? Even in the coldest regions, crabapples can be relied on for sumptuous displays of pink, white and red. The impact of

these early-flowering trees is compounded because they flower while the emerging leaves are still insignificant.

Later in spring and through the summer, blossoms are enhanced by lush foliage. Yellow flower clusters hang below fresh young leaves on golden chain trees (*Laburnum* × *Watereri*). Stewartias follow, with white camellialike flowers nestled among light green foliage. In midsummer, Japanese pagoda (*Sophora japonica*) take center stage with creamy white pealike flowers against deep green leaves. The large white flowers of bullbays, or southern magnolias (*Magnolia grandiflora*), are deliciously lemon scented and sit singly among

the large evergreen foliage like white doves. Mimosas (*Albizia Julibrissin*) are curiously tropical in appearance with their pink brushlike flowers among the lacy light green leaves, providing a long display during the warmest months. The sourwoods (*Oxydendron arboreum*) also have a long display. Their small white flowers, along pendant stems, appear in early summer, but give way to creamy seedpods that effectively continue the display through summer. Latest to bloom, from August to October, are Franklin trees (*Franklinia Alatamaha*), also with white camellialike flowers. Their final flowers open as the leaves change to crimson. The flowers of lindens (*Tilia* species) are

In cool climates, where golden chain trees, Laburnum × Watereri, *grow well, they can be trained over an arch, through which their pendant flower clusters hang. This is the laburnum arch at Barnsley House, England.*

The summer-flowering hardy silk tree, Albizia Julibrissin, *has a tropical appearance.*

not particularly showy, but their summer fragrance is a not-to-be-forgotten experience. Although summer-blooming trees are not as common as spring bloomers, they need not be in short supply in the landscape.

In the North, autumn- and winter-flowering trees are few. But they are scarcely needed, because the winter landscape is rich with colorful fruit, waxy, colored twigs and textured bark. As spring is the season of flowers, so autumn is the season of fruit. More berries and fruit ripen at this season than any other. Depending on the variety of tree, some will ripen early among green foliage and remain as the foliage assumes the tints of autumn. Others color later, along with the foliage, which makes some remarkable contrasts. Many trees retain their fruit in such profusion after the leaves have fallen that they create a major visual impact in the winter garden. Fruits can be red, orange, yellow, blue or nearly black. Bright colors are preferred by humans because they show up better in the autumn or winter landscape, but wildlife seek out black and blue berries as winter food. Crabapples (_Malus_ species) are among the most valuable trees bearing decorative fruit; they have a range of colors, some varieties hold their fruit until spring, and they can be grown in most regions of North America. Mountain ashes (_Sorbus Aucuparia_) have some of the showiest fruit of all trees, but do best in the North where summers are cool. Farther south, idesias (_Idesia polycarpa_) are good substitutes for mountain ashes, with sim-

ilar clusters of fruit. Evergreen hollies (_Ilex_ species) are small trees with red berries. Autumn arrangements of cut branches of foliage and fruit can be as striking as flowers and more in keeping with the season.

Cones of pines (_Pinus_ species), spruces (_Picea_ species) and other conifers often remain attractive for the whole year, because many kinds continue to hang on the tree for indefinite periods. Cones come in all sizes from less than an inch to a foot long. Immature cones may take on attractive colors during the growing season, such as those of Korean firs (_Abies koreana_), which become a striking purple. Through the summer, slender, pendant green cones hang from the branches of eastern white pines (_Pinus Strobus_). And in the winter, use mature cones, in all their variety, for holiday decorations indoors.

Through the winter, dried capsules and papery fruit catch the snow and rustle in the wind. The swollen papery capsules of goldenrain trees (_Koelreuteria paniculata_) hang in great clusters, while the smaller capsules of sourwoods continue to cling to their pendant stems until spring.

Color and contrast in the winter landscape are not confined to berries and cones. White trunks of birches (_Betula_ species) stand out so prominently that they catch the eye and make it stop—they punctuate views. Up close, the papery, cinnamon-colored bark of paperbark maples (_Acer griseum_) joins with ordinary evergreens for an extraordinary composition. Lacebark pines (_Pinus Bungeana_)

The lacy beauty of European larch, Larix decidua, _a deciduous conifer, is highlighted by ice and snow._

provide their own evergreen foliage as an interesting counterpoint to bark mottled with gray-brown, olive and tan. Twigs of some trees assume bright colors especially for the winter season. Those of golden weeping willows (_Salix alba tristis_) glow against a blue sky. Some upright willows are grown for their twigs that become red or orange with the onset of winter. Only the youngest twigs have the striking color, so these trees are often pollarded, or cut short, each spring to encourage vigorous growth. No one could forget the spectacle of coral bark maple (_Acer palmatum_ 'Senkaki') in the snow. Contorted willows (_Salix Matsudana_ 'Tortuosa') and Japanese cut-leaf maples (_Acer palmatum dissectum_ varieties) show off their fascinating twisted branches best after the leaves have fallen. Planted in front of a wall, their shadows cast a silhouette that changes throughout the day as the sun moves across the sky.

Nevertheless, foliage is still the single most important characteristic of trees. In the garden,

Eastern white pine, Pinus Strobus, _bears attractive cones._

In addition to the pastel yellow and sometimes orange, autumn tints of katsura tree, Cercidiphyllum japonicum, *the freshly fallen leaves also have a delicious burnt-sugar fragrance.*

foliage has the longest-lasting impact on the landscape. Foliage is also the part of the tree with which we are most familiar. Show someone a maple leaf, and chances are, he or she can identify it. Show someone a piece of bark, a twig or even a single flower, and chances are he or she will be lost.

From the first emerging leaves of spring, foliage is a changing feature through the year. The fresh green of the first tiny willow leaves and the reddish tints of red maple leaves along the roadside are welcome sights. These early colors lose their intensity or fade to green in summer, but some trees retain interesting foliage color all summer long. For regions with cool summers, golden black locusts (*Robinia Pseudoacacia* 'Frisia') are unsurpassed for their yellow foliage. Trees with reddish foliage are more common, and include bloodgood Japanese maples (*Acer palmatum* 'Bloodgood'), purpleleaf plums (*Prunus cerasifera* 'Thundercloud'), crimson king maples (*Acer platanoides* 'Crimson King') and European purple beeches (*Fagus sylvatica* 'Atropunicea').

Variegated foliage in trees is often regarded as gaudy, but can be attractive if it is clean looking and if the tree is sited well in the landscape. In hot climates, variegated plants are more subject to foliage burn than their all-green counterparts. Some are tough enough, though, to be used in most regions where they are hardy. One form of Norway maple (*Acer platanoides* 'Drummondii') has a clean white edge around each leaf. There is a variety of tulip tree (*Liriodendron Tulipifera* 'Aureo-marginatum') with a yellow edge to each leaf. Several different kinds of flowering dogwood are now available with variegated foliage. Any branches reverting to normal green foliage must be pruned out of variegated trees, because these are often more vigorous and tend to take over.

The transition to winter is a time for great change in foliage. Many trees exhibit brilliant or clear pastel colors before shedding their leaves. The renowned October oranges and yellows of sugar maples throughout New England is testament to this phenomenon. Just as trees are planted in gardens for their flowers, they are also planted for their autumn tints, particularly in regions where fall colors are normally dull. Black gums (*Nyssa sylvatica*), Katsura trees (*Cercidiphyllum japonicum*), red maples (*Acer rubrum*), Japanese maples (*Acer palmatum*), sourwoods (*Oxydendron arboreum*), scarlet oaks (*Quercus coccinea*), sweet gums (*Liquidambar Styraciflua*) and golden larches (*Pseudolarix amabilis*) are just a few of the trees planted especially for this purpose. Even the foliage of some so-called evergreens take on reddish or golden tints in winter. One form of Japanese cedar (*Cryptomeria japonica* 'Elegans') assumes a reddish coloration as the weather cools.

TREES IN NATURE

Observing trees in nature will help you understand their place in your garden. In nature most trees grow in forests or with other trees. In a mature forest, young trees grow up among the older trees to replace those that die. A mature forest is called a "climax" forest and the young trees that grow there are able to grow in the shade of other trees. Oaks, tulip trees and hemlocks typically grow in such forests, where individuals of all ages can be seen together. Mature forests have smaller "understory" trees, ones that never become large. These small trees spend their entire lives in the shade, and many, including the dogwood, flower spectacularly. Other trees, such as birches, will not grow in the shade. These "pioneer" trees are found growing in open fields that are reverting to forest. Once the forest is established, they die out.

Trees that grow on slopes or in well-drained soils will probably suffer in wet, poorly drained locations. Others, such as willows, bald cypresses and red maples, grow best where they have wet feet. Those found thriving at the top of a hill are probably fairly tolerant of drought and dry conditions. Many kinds of pines grow in such dry locations.

How well you match a tree to the conditions of the planting site will determine your chances of success. You can plant most shade-tolerant climax trees in the sun, but you won't succeed with a pioneer species planted in the shade. If you have a sunny property, there is a wide choice of trees from which to choose. If you have a wooded property and want to add more trees, a birch won't grow but a young oak will. To add more color, plant such understory flowering trees as dogwood, Japanese snowbells and stewartias, rather than crabapples, which prefer more sun. Surprising as it may seem, you can even have trees in a low wet spot—if you make the right choice.

Cypress knees develop from the roots of bald cypress, Taxodium distichum, *when it grows in wet, swampy soils.*

What to Look For:

DESIRABLE QUALITIES

Small leaves or leaflets, don't need raking (honey locust)

Leathery leaves, make good mulch without packing down (oak)

Small, attractive fruit that does not become messy (callery pear, crabapple)

Disease and pest resistant (katsura tree)

Deep roots compatible with other plantings (oak)

Neat habits—doesn't constantly drop leaves, bark, branches (katsura tree)

UNDESIRABLE QUALITIES

Shallow roots (Norway maple, plane tree, linden)

Roots apt to grow into and clog sewer lines (willow, poplar)

Large soft leaves that smother small plants and bulbs (London plane tree)

SHED DEBRIS ALL SUMMER

Leaves (many trees)

Bark (London plane tree, white oak)

Branches and twigs (tulip tree, white oak)

SHED NUISANCE FRUIT

Spiney (Chinese chestnut, horse chestnut)

Smelly (female ginkgo)

Large pods (honey locust, catalpa)

Toxic to other plants (black walnut)

DISEASE AND PEST SUSCEPTIBLE

Aphids (tulip tree, linden)

Borers (mountain ash, many birches)

Leaf miner (American holly, birch)

Dutch elm disease (American elm)

THE PLANTING AND GROWING GUIDE

HOW TREES GROW

The most commonly asked questions about tree care refer to the proper times for fertilizing, pruning and planting, and the answers call for a basic knowledge of how trees grow. Despite the wide variety of tree types, all grow in pretty much the same way. Extension growth occurs at the ends of both shoots and roots, where the tips have zones of actively dividing cells called meristems. Trunks do not stretch, and a branch will not become higher above the ground with age. Trunks thicken from the cambium, a layer of actively dividing cells under the bark. The cambium lays down new rings of wood, which thicken the trunk, and new layers of bark. The wood inside the cambium conducts water and nutrients up to the leaves where they are transformed into sugars, the tree's food, by photosynthesis. These sugars are taken down to the roots by the phloem, located under the bark outside the cambium layer.

The growth cycle of trees is regulated by the length of the days at different seasons. Shortening days of late summer and autumn signal preparation for winter dormancy and the formation of leaf buds for the following year. Once dormant, trees have a cold requirement that must be satisfied before the tree can grow again. This cold requirement, different for different trees, simply is the number of consecutive days when the temperature is below a critical level, usually around 40°F. A tree will not have normal spring growth unless it has had enough cold days the preceding winter. This is a safeguard for the tree against leafing out in an early warm spell and then being damaged by the return of cold weather. Northern trees have longer cold requirements than southern variants, one reason many northern trees don't grow well in the Deep South. With the coming of spring, longer days and warmer temperatures stimulate growth until the shorter days of mid- and late summer signal growth to slow down again. Different kinds of trees have different bloom seasons because they produce flowers in response to different day lengths.

A tree's metabolism changes with the seasons. Although trees might be able to withstand bitterly cold temperatures in midwinter, even a light frost in summer can cause severe damage. In spring, soft tissues and low starch reserves render trees most susceptible to pest and disease attacks. The cool seasons of fall, winter and spring are the periods of most active root growth. These seasons are the best times to plant and transplant trees because lost roots are quickly and easily replaced when the starch reserves needed to grow roots are at their highest. It's also a good time because dormant trees have lower moisture requirements. The best times to fertilize trees are late fall and early spring, when the developing roots absorb nutrients in

The great majority of trees flower in spring, as does this May-blooming red buckeye, Aesculus Pavia, *a small native tree.*

preparation for spring growth.

Perhaps the least understood aspect of a tree is the root system. It is not the same shape as the top, and does not go as deep as the tree is high, as some people may believe. In fact, most feeder roots are in the top few inches of soil, where most nutrients are, and they spread farther than the branches. Well-drained and aerated soil will encourage roots to grow more deeply, adding to the strength and drought tolerance of the tree.

In spite of the covering of snow on this Canadian hemlock, Tsuga canadensis, *its roots may still be active below ground.*

OBTAINING TREES

Once you've decided what types of trees to plant, the next step is to obtain them. Most any tree you want is available from a nursery somewhere. You'll find the most popular kinds for your area at local nurseries and garden centers. If you shop around a bit you can get the best values in a range of sizes to suit your budget. Both rare and very new varieties are usually available only from specialty nurseries, and most of these are mail order. Local nurseries offer trees in any of three ways. The smaller sizes are available in pots or containers. The largest containers can hold sizable landscape specimens, but large trees are usually balled-and-burlapped, often termed "B&B." (These trees have been field grown and dug with a ball of the field soil around the roots.

This ball is wrapped in burlap and tied with rope to hold it together.) A really large landscape specimen must be dug and transplanted with a mechanical tree spade. Very large trees are always expensive, and purchasing them is not necessarily the quickest way to get a big tree, because they take longer to resume normal growth rate and become fully established. A smaller tree will become established faster, and may actually outgrow the large transplant.

Mail-order nurseries supply smaller trees due to the limitations and expense of shipping. But it is often worth the several years' wait for that extra-special variety to grow. Because you can't see the mail-order merchandise before you buy, check the guarantees of quality and customer satisfaction and buy

from reputable mail-order firms. The smallest trees are sent in containers, but larger deciduous broad-leaved trees are often sent bareroot. This saves on postage and enables you to get a larger plant. Planting bareroot trees is not risky if it is done at the correct time. Many nursery owners believe that planting bareroot trees is preferable to planting balled-and-burlapped trees. The exposed roots can be spread more easily, thereby coming into direct contact with the soil in which they are to live. Experts feel that root growth is inhibited by a change from one kind of soil to another, particularly when the new soil is poorer; this is the case when roots must grow forth from a rich potting soil into field soil.

WHEN TO PLANT

Container-grown trees can be planted at just about any time that you can buy them—year 'round where winters are mild. It's best to avoid planting in very warm weather, however. Bareroot trees must be planted when dormant, before the leaves appear. Many can be planted in fall; some should be planted only in spring. Your nursery

will supply them at the correct time for planting. The advantage of planting in the fall or as early in spring as possible is that the new tree has plenty of time to spread its roots into new soil before summer, a time of potential drought and a time when trees can rapidly dehydrate. Summer is the season when most newly planted trees

die. Trees planted in late spring and summer need more attentive watering.

Once you have purchased or received your trees they must be held in good condition until they can be planted. Mail-order plants (particularly evergreens or anything in leaf) should be opened immediately on arrival to check on their condition and allow air to get to the tops. Without air circulation and light, the foliage is susceptible to disease and mold. The soil or packing material around the roots of bareroot trees should be moistened if dry and then rewrapped. All trees are best kept out of strong light and in a cold place until planted, but they should be protected from freezing temperatures. Under these conditions, bareroot trees can easily be kept for a week or so if checked regularly. Container-grown trees are more easily cared for because their roots are established in the pots. They can be kept outdoors until planting, provided they are kept moist and protected from freezing temperatures and hungry animals.

SOIL PREPARATION

Good soil preparation is the first step to planting. The most important task is to reduce compaction by breaking up the soil as thoroughly as possible. Break up the soil when it is moderately moist or dry, so that it crumbles, never when it is wet and sticky because it will become more compacted. Usually, it is best not to loosen the soil deeper than the depth of the root ball or pot, or else the tree may sink too deeply when the soil settles later. If you do loosen the soil in the bottom of the hole more deeply, use your foot to press it down again. Your body weight is about the right pressure to settle the soil properly without unwanted compaction.

Experts used to recommend adding such soil amendments as leaf mold, peat moss and sand to improve the soil around the roots of a new tree. This is no longer advocated. It is impractical to improve all the soil into which a tree's roots will eventually extend, of course, and just a pocket of amended soil discourages roots from growing into the surrounding, unimproved soil. It would be like planting the tree in a big pot. It reduces drought resistance and, therefore, the tree's chances of survival. Merely loosening the soil thoroughly is enough to encourage strong root growth.

The danger of root strangulation cannot be overemphasized. The effects may not become evident for several years, when the tree becomes sick and dies. Grown commercially, young trees often become pot bound or their roots are crammed into the ground in such a way that they get twisted around the trunk or each other. This can cause some roots to encircle other roots or the trunk. As the tree grows, these encircling roots kill the tree by cutting off sap flow. Straightening or removing encircling roots at planting is the best corrective treatment, and will not threaten the life of the tree. If you provide good aftercare, the tree can easily recover from the loss of even a quarter of its roots.

Planting a Container-grown or Bareroot Tree

1. Be sure tree is not dehydrated. Water containers the day before planting or soak roots of bareroot tree in water overnight. Keep all roots moist at all times.

2. Dig hole at least twice as wide as the pot or root ball, but not deeper.

3. Mound soil in bottom of hole high enough for tree to sit so soil level from nursery or pot is about 2 inches above the surrounding soil level. As the tree settles, this prevents a depression from forming that can collect water and cause root or crown rot in compacted or poorly drained soils.

4. Remove tree from pot or wrapping and set in hole.

5. Orient tree for best side to face forward.

6. Loosen soil around sides and bottom of root ball.

7. Trim all damaged or dead roots back to healthy tissue with clean cuts to stimulate new root growth.

8. Spread roots over mound, including encircling and matted roots, to promote growth into new soil and prevent root strangulation. Remove encircling roots that can't be spread.

9. Install stakes outside diameter of root ball as required to support tree.

10. Backfill hole, spreading roots in layers.

11. Firm soil in hole with foot.

12. Form soil basin, at least as wide as hole, to contain irrigation water, so when you water the tree, the water will soak in before it runs off.

13. Apply mulch 2 to 3 inches deep to prevent moisture loss, cracking of dried soil surface and competition from grass and weeds.

14. Secure tree to stakes with appropriate ties.

15. Water thoroughly.

Planting a Balled-and-burlapped Tree

1. Be sure tree is not dehydrated. Water thoroughly the day before planting.

2. Dig hole at least twice as wide as root ball, but not deeper.

3. Set tree in hole so soil level from nursery is about 2 inches above the surrounding soil level. As the tree settles, this prevents a depression from forming that can collect water and cause root or crown rot in compacted or poorly drained soils.

4. Orient tree for best side to face forward.

5. Remove rope or twine around trunk and top of ball.

6. Natural fiber burlap may be left around the roots of the tree, but it must be folded down into hole or cut away. None must be exposed above the soil because it acts like a wick to dry the soil and roots. All synthetic or plastic twine and burlap must be removed to prevent strangulation.

7. Check for encircling and strangulation roots. This may require temporarily removing soil on

surface of ball to examine major roots at the base of the trunk.

8. Trim all damaged or dead roots back to healthy tissue with clean cuts to stimulate new root growth.

9. Spread encircling and matted roots to promote growth into new soil and prevent strangulation. Remove encircling roots that can't be spread.

10. Install stakes outside diameter of root ball as required to support tree.

11. Backfill hole, spreading roots in layers.

12. Firm soil in hole with foot.

13. Form soil basin, at least as wide as hole, to contain irrigation water, so when you water the tree, the water will soak in before it runs off.

14. Apply mulch 2 to 3 inches deep to prevent moisture loss, cracking of dried soil surface and competition from grass and weeds.

15. Secure tree to stakes with appropriate ties.

16. Water thoroughly.

STAKING

Young trees are staked for two reasons. Staking supports the tree and prevents it from leaning or being uprooted until it is strong enough to stand on its own. It protects a tree from damage by lawn mowers, other machinery or vehicles and people. Generally, it is best to provide support only when necessary, for as short a period as possible. Some trees, including smaller bareroot trees and conifers branched low to the ground, do not need staking at all. High trees with a long trunk and wide top, or those in locations subject to strong winds, nearly always need to be staked.

Stakes should be installed at the time of planting, before you fill the hole, to avoid damage to the tree roots. Use two or three stakes, and place them outside the diameter of the root ball. Almost any material can be used for stakes, including old metal pipes, "T" fence stakes, rebar (concrete reinforcement rods) and wooden poles up to 2 inches in diameter (for large trees).

Ties must not damage the bark and should allow the trunk to move. Bark injury can result in the death of the top of the

tree, and trunks tied too tightly are subject to breakage at the point of attachment. Wire covered with pieces of old hose are the most common materials used for large trees, but not the best. Experts recommend the use of soft materials such as rubber or canvas straps, which are less damaging to the bark. Make broad loops between each of the stakes and the trunk or use a figure eight, rather than a smaller loop around the trunk. Keep in mind that trunks thicken and strengthen faster when they can move freely. The stakes and ties can usually be removed after a year.

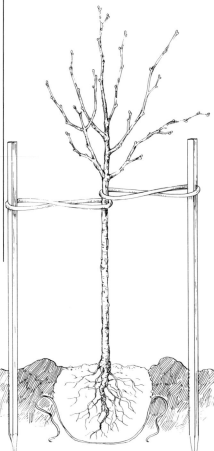

A newly planted tree that needs staking should be secured at the lowest height that will still hold it in place. Wide straps, tied loosely in a figure-eight, will adequately support the trunk yet avoid damaging it.

TREE CARE

Watering is the most important concern for a newly planted tree in its first year, especially in the summer. Most regions are subject to at least one period of drought each year, and this can kill or seriously damage a new tree. A neighbor of mine once asked about his conifers, planted about a year before, that had lost their tops. This was almost certainly due to lack of water during a summer dry spell. Drought-damaged trees may or may not recover. Check your trees weekly, and if need be, dig down into the original root ball to make sure the soil is moist. If it's not, water deeply immediately. Don't be fooled by a light rain—it will only make a fool out of you. At least 1 inch of rain, maybe more depending on your soil, is required to wet the whole root area deeply enough to satisfy your tree.

Even for established trees, the general rule is that they need 1 inch of rain per week. Most established trees can easily survive intermittent dry spells, but keep an eye on them for signs that they want some help. Watch for drooping leaves or wilting that does not recover once the sun is off the foliage.

If you live in an arid region, you can either plant trees adapted to your climate or commit yourself to regular watering for the life of the tree. With water becoming scarcer in many regions, it is much wiser to plant drought-tolerant trees. Even if you are willing to water, you may not be permitted to because of shortages. If you live in an arid region, you may be fortunate enough to have a native tree or two already on your property. Be aware that these trees are not adapted to having additonal irrigation. If you water a lawn around these trees, the extra water is likely to cause a root rot and the trees may die as in the case of many California live oaks. It is an all-too-common scenario in which fine old specimens needing little care are killed by ignorance and replaced by trees needing more water and care.

MULCHING

There are few situations where mulch is not beneficial. Mulch is put on top of the ground, not dug in. In time, organic mulches break down into fine, dark humus. Most trees are adapted to growing with something covering the soil; indeed, the litter on a forest floor is a natural mulch. Mulch maintains moisture in the soil, adds organic matter and nutrients, and helps keep the soil cooler in summer and warmer in winter. Mulch also allows more water to penetrate the soil by preserving the porosity of the surface and holding water in place so it can soak in. By slowing runoff, it reduces soil erosion. If you are looking to save work, remember that a good mulch will suppress weeds very effectively without the toxicity of herbicides.

The best kinds of mulch for trees are wood chips and bark. These will last for a year or two. Grass clippings can also be used in moderation and are a good source of nitrogen. Pine needles (straw) and stiff leathery leaves of such trees as oaks make a good mulch, because they will not pack down. Maple leaves are less suitable because they are too soft and a thick layer may mat down on the soil, restricting aeration.

Use mulch properly. You will often see trees with 6 or more inches of mulch around them. This is a labor-saving technique that can have fatal results. Overmulching can keep the soil too wet, reduce aeration, encourage some diseases and even prevent water from reaching the soil. It also provides a home for hungry mice that can damage bark. The proper depth for a bark or wood-chip mulch is about 3 inches. A loose leafy mulch can be deeper because it will settle. Remember that the need to replace mulch is a good sign. It is being broken down into nutrients that your tree can use.

GROUNDCOVERS

A groundcover planting is a natural way to complete your landscape because it acts as a living mulch, and helps to hold a mulch of leaves in place. Grass is less suitable, especially around young trees, because it competes vigorously with tree roots for water and nutrients. A groundcover under the drip line of your tree will promote the tree's health and vigor. Good groundcover subjects are *Pachysandra* and *Vinca*. English ivy will survive among the toughest roots of such trees as Norway maples and lindens, but it is too competitive for best growth of other trees.

PRUNING AND TRAINING

Pruning is one of the most useful techniques for shaping a tree and controlling growth. It can also prevent future problems. It is an art that warrants extensive study, but its principles are quite simple. "Apical dominance" is a term that describes the influence of the tip of a shoot over the buds and side branches below it. The terminal bud suppresses, or limits, the growth of side buds below it. The strength of apical dominance is partly determined by the plant species. Trees with strong apical dominance have a single leader and horizontal side branches below it, as do most conifers. Trees with weaker apical dominance lack a single strong leader and have many upright branches, as with many broad-leaved trees. Terminal buds on side branches perform a similar function, suppressing the growth of buds immediately behind them. When a terminal bud is damaged or pruned off, dominance is broken and several side buds come into growth. One or more of these will begin to behave as terminals. It is for this reason that frequent pruning makes a plant more bushy. If it is indiscriminately done, however, the natural shape of the plant will be lost. When pruning is properly done, a plant's shape can be corrected and its health improved.

Young trees should be lightly pruned to shape them for the future. For spreading broad-leaved trees, select and keep strong, evenly spaced scaffold branches. These branches will determine the basic shape of the tree. Remove rubbing and crossing branches that will cause wounds subject to infection. Suckers and branches that point in toward the center of the tree should also be pruned out. Avoid narrow crotches as they are structurally weak and apt to break away when the tree gets bigger, leaving a wound that is difficult to heal. Narrow crotches

Young trees usually need some pruning to encourage them to develop a strong branch structure. First, prune out any dead or damaged branches. Next, remove the smaller or less shapely leaders when there is more than one. Finally, cut out any rubbing branches to prevent worn bark, an invitation to insects and disease. The upper branches and ultimate leader indicate the shape of the mature tree.

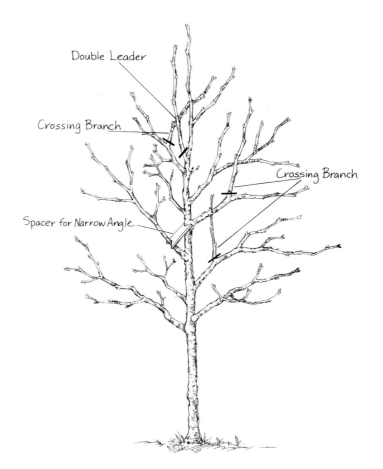

Double Leader

Crossing Branch

Crossing Branch

Spacer for Narrow Angle

in young trees can be widened with a spreader to increase the angle between the branch and the trunk. A spreader is nothing more than a dowel or stick, with a notch in each end, that is wedged in the crotch. The branch will take the shape in which it is held after a year or so (depending on the size of the branch). Remove competing leaders. For a strong tree, even broad-leaved trees that will ultimately develop several leaders should be held to a single leader when young. Conifers need virtually no scaffold pruning, but they should always be kept to a single leader.

Shaping a tree doesn't have to be accomplished in one year, nor must all nonscaffold branches be removed from the start. The more branches you leave on the tree, the more leaves it will have for photosynthesis, the stronger it will be and the faster it will grow. Leaving small branches along the trunk will help to thicken and strengthen it. These can be removed without harm in future years.

When to Prune

If you have just planted a tree, you will probably want to trim a few branches to shape it. But you should leave major pruning until winter or early spring, when the tree is dormant. During dormancy a tree has its highest food reserves stored for the spring flush of growth. Pruning during the dormant season simply rechannels the energy, causing different buds to grow. When you remove leaves during the summer, you take away some of the tree's ability to make and store food. It can be useful, however, if you are pruning to control size.

Peculiarities of different tree types influence the ideal time to prune. Cherries, elms, birches and maples tend to bleed from fresh cuts made in the spring, so they should be pruned in fall. Bleeding is not usually harmful to the tree, but it is alarming to the gardener and can hinder healing or encourage certain infections if it is prolonged. Evergreens are best pruned shortly before growth begins, because they can use their foliage to photosynthesize at a reduced level during the winter, adding strength to the plant. There is also the danger of winter damage to bark suddenly exposed to winter sun when the evergreen branches shading it are removed. Otherwise, prune most trees anytime during the winter, when there is little else to keep you busy in the garden.

How to Prune

Removal of a branch of any size opens a wound that increases risk of infection by fungi, bacteria and insects. The size and kind of wound are factors that influence the tree's ability to resist infection. Small cuts heal quickly and pose little risk. The larger the cut, the higher the risk of infection before the wound heals over. Soft-wooded trees are more prone to rot. You can help the tree by making the cut properly.

Dr. Alex Shigo spent 25 years with the United States Forest Service, wounding and dissecting trees to discover how they become infected and heal. He recommends that all branches be cut where the branch meets the collar, a swollen area at its base. The collar has an increased resistance to infection, and it has the ability to isolate infection to keep it from spreading. If you cut close to the trunk and remove or damage the collar, you leave the tree defenseless. Experts used to recommend "flush cuts," but these are now considered harmful by Dr. Shigo and others. Nor should stubs be left beyond the collar, as the tree cannot heal them over, and they provide an ideal entry point for infections.

Removal of large branches with a saw involves the risk of tearing the bark down the trunk. To prevent this, make three cuts. The first cut should be several inches out from the collar from the underside of the branch for about a third of its diameter. Then make a second cut from above, just beyond the undercut, until the branch breaks off. This will leave you with a short stub that can be safely cut at the proper point without the risk of its weight tearing the bark. Dr. Shigo says that you can tell a good cut by the way that it heals. The healing wood should form evenly around the whole cut like a donut, not thicker in some areas. When removing dead branches, cut back to the living bark, but do not cut into or damage it.

Wound dressings on tree cuts are a controversial subject, but are no longer recommended by Dr. Shigo. He says that the environment of the wood sealed under the dressing is ideal for infectious organisms.

The London plane tree, Platanus × aceri- folia, *is commonly used in* allée *plantings in Europe, where it is pruned regularly to maintain a uniform size. This is the famous* allée *at the Jardin des Plantes, Paris.*

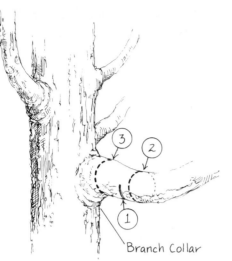

Branch Collar

To cut a large branch: First, make a partial cut from the underside, about 4 or 5 inches from the branch collar; this will prevent the branch from tearing the bark down the trunk. Next, make a cut from above, beyond the first cut. Now, make the final cut next to the branch collar.

The practice of topping mature trees (indiscriminately cutting off the tops of trees) is a despicable one. It has been likened to a haircut, but it is more accurately compared with cutting off an arm somewhere between the wrist and elbow. The problem with this kind of pruning is that when the top of a trunk is cut off, there is no branch collar to fight infection and it moves directly down into the heart of the tree. Topping also forces many weakly attached shoots to form around the decayed stumps. Many of these will grow into large branches that can snap off at their bases. As decay progresses down through the tree, it seldom shows external symptoms, but the structure of the tree is continuously weakened, leading to unexpected breakage in the future.

There are several alternatives to topping trees. The most sensible is to choose trees that will not outgrow their spaces. However, many problem trees are already in place. Rather than shortening the tree to below utility lines, it can be pruned to grow around them, with the wires passing through the center. In the long run, this is cheaper, because it requires less frequent maintenance. If you are concerned about a tree hanging over your house, shorten branches back to forks and crotches that can heal quickly or remove only particularly large branches that hang directly over the house. Such steps reduce the risk of damage from the tree, while simultaneously preserving its shade and aesthetic value.

Seek the services and advice of a reputable tree surgeon for such work. Tree climbing is dangerous and should only be attempted by trained professionals.

Trimming small branches and shaping with hand pruners is a simple procedure. When removing a whole branch, don't leave stubs but rather cut back to the swelling at the base of the branch. When shortening a shoot or twig, make the cut about a quarter inch above a bud. Cut back to a bud that points in the direction that you want the branch to grow. Buds at the ends of side branches should point out or down, whereas those on a leader should point up.

When the terminal or leader of a tree is damaged or destroyed, a new one may be slow to form, especially in conifers. To reestablish a new leader, tie a side branch into a vertical position until it becomes fixed there, and begins to behave like a leader. It may take a year or two for the adjustment. If several leaders form, remove all but the one that is strongest and in the best position.

FERTILIZING TREES

Fertilization of trees is another controversial topic. Advice differs on how, when and what nutrients are most important. One point of agreement is that fertilization is not a universal cure-all for poor or compacted soil, bad drainage, excessive shade or a tree that is ill-suited to its environment. Many trees grow and thrive for years without any fertilizing. Under ideal conditions, where trees have a natural mulch and groundcover, or grow in woodland conditions, fertilizer is rarely necessary. A great way to simulate these conditions is to spread compost under your trees. Many trees, however, are grown in situations where naturally occuring nutrients, in the form of leaves, are swept away and their roots must compete with voracious grass roots. These trees may benefit from fertilization. In other cases, a specific symptom, such as off-color foliage, indicates the need to correct a nutrient deficiency.

The three nutrients that plants need in greatest quantity are nitrogen (N), phosphorus (P) and potassium (K). The analysis of a fertilizer is given on the package as percentages of these nutrients in a series of three numbers. For example, 10-6-4 means 10 percent N, 6 percent

P and 4 percent K. (The remaining percentage is mostly inert ingredients.) Such other nutrients as iron, boron and magnesium are required in much smaller quantities and are termed micronutrients, or trace elements. They are less often included in standard fertilizers and applied only when specifically called for due to local soil conditions or to correct symptoms, for which an expert should be consulted. Too high a concentration of trace elements can be toxic to some plants.

Fertilizing is often termed "feeding," but this is an inaccurate description. Fertilizer only supplies nutrients. The nutrients are transformed by photosynthesis into sugars and starches, the tree's real food. The easiest method of application is to broadcast dry, granular fertilizer on the surface of the soil or lawn. (Be sure to do it when grass and foliage are dry, or it may burn the plants because it will stick to wet foliage.) As most feeder roots are shallow, they will pick up the nutrients. Fertilizing is best done in late fall to early spring, for two reasons. First, grass and other plants are dormant at these times and less likely to absorb the fertilizer before the trees get it. Second, the tree roots are actively absorbing and storing nutrients in preparation for the spring flush of growth, when they are most needed. Don't fertilize when the soil is frozen; it is likely to get washed off rather than absorbed, and tree roots are not active when the soil temperature is below about 40°F.

You may wonder why many arborists fertilize trees by drilling holes in the soil and why it is not recommended here. The theory behind fertilizing in holes is that it puts the nutrients below the depth of other plant roots where only the tree can get them. We feel that placing fertilizer in holes is unnecessary, because feeder roots are shallow. It is also more difficult for the homeowner to do.

Blanket recommendations about how much fertilizer and what specific nutrients to apply are impossible to give. It depends on your soil and the conditions under which the tree is grown. First consider the health of your trees. Are they growing well? Is the foliage a healthy color? Are there any pest problems? It may be that no fertilizer is necessary. Next, get a soil test. Soil tests are often provided through your state cooperative extension service. Inquire at local nurseries, garden centers and public gardens about how to get a soil test in your area. The results will recommend a treatment for your soil conditions. General rates on a fertilizer bag will tell you how much of that formulation can be safely applied without harming your tree, but this will not reflect your tree's actual need. There is also debate as to whether trees should be fertilized in their first year. Certainly it is not advisable to push newly planted trees too fast, before their root systems are established enough to support such growth. Most experts agree that when you fertilize, a slow-release fertilizer is better because it releases nutrients gradually so the tree can use them more efficiently. There is no doubt that it is far more important to keep the trees watered when newly planted. Fertilizing your trees is just one of several things you can do to increase their health and vigor, which in turn helps them to resist pests and diseases and perhaps grow faster for a quicker landscape effect.

The grand southern live oak, Quercus virginiana, *live to great ages and develop strong, wide-spreading branches.*

PLANT PORTRAITS

PLANT PORTRAIT KEY

Scientific names of trees are in boldface italics. They are essential for precision when discussing specific trees. Common names vary so much from region to region that readers and nursery owners alike cannot be sure what tree to plant. Scientific names can tell you something about the plants by showing their relationships to each other.

They are usually based on Latin or Greek, languages that don't change and so will always be understood internationally. Each name is a subdivision of the former. The first name is the genus (plural, genera), which is always capitalized. The second name is the species, which need not be capitalized, although some botanists will capitalize it if it is derived from a proper noun, such as a person's name (i.e., *Chamaecyparis Lawsoniana*, the Lawson cypress). These names are in italics. All plants have at least two botanical names.

Additional names may be added to designate a variety, subspecies or a cultivar. A variety usually occurs naturally, in the wild. It is written in the same way as the species name. *Cultivar* means *culti*vated *vari*ety and is a variant created or found only in gardens. The name is usually a modern-language name, is not italicized, is always capitalized and is placed in single quotes (i.e., the Japanese maple cultivar 'Bloodgood').

Many garden trees are hybrids. This may be indicated in the name by an "×" (but it is not required). The position of the × tells you what has been hybridized. When placed before the species name, × tells you that it is a hybrid between two other species. Saucer magnolia (*Magnolia* ×*Soulangiana*) is a hybrid of Yulan magnolia (*M. denudata*) and lily magnolia (*M. liliiflora*). It might be explained this way: *Magnolia* ×*Soulangiana* (*M. denudata* × *M. liliiflora*). It is also possible, but less common, to have hybrids between two genera, which is indicated by placing the × before the name of the genus. Leyland cypress is the only example in this book: ×*Cupressocyparis Leylandii* (*Cupressus macrocarpa* × *Chamaecyparis nootkatensis*). There are many hybrid cultivars.

Unfortunately, there is sometimes more than one scientific name for the same tree. One name is considered to be more correct than the others. When other names are in common use, the synonyms are given in parentheses immediately following the preferred name.

Phonetic pronunciation of the scientific name is in parentheses.

Common name of tree is in boldface type.

Primary ornamental features: the most important features of a tree. These are found directly after the common name in lightface type.

Seasons of bloom: SP = Spring, SU = Summer, F = Fall, E = Early, M = Middle, L = Late, i.e., ESP = Early Spring

The average hours of sun needed per day is indicated by symbols. The first symbol is what the tree prefers, but the tree is adaptable to all conditions listed.

The deodar cedar, Cedrus Deodara, *from the Himalayas, makes a graceful specimen.*

○ Sun: 6 hours or more of strong direct sunlight per day.

◐ Part Shade: 3 to 6 hours of direct sunlight, light dappled shade all day or high shade all day. (High shade means that the shade is cast by high branches, allowing plenty of diffuse, indirect light to come from the sides.)

● Shade: 2 hours or less of direct sunlight, relatively dark locations. Few trees work as specimens in full shade.

Life Span (approximate):

▉ **Short:** less than 60 years

▉ **Moderate:** 60 to 120 years

▉ **Long:** More than 120 years

▉ **Very long:** approximately 1,000 years or more

Zones: Hardiness zones are derived from The USDA Plant Hardiness Map (pages 92–93). This map is based on average minimum winter temperatures, the most important factor determining hardiness. Other factors affect plant survival and health, too. High summer temperatures in the Southeast may kill or limit a plant's growth, whereas the same plant will grow successfully in the cooler summers of an equivalent zone of winter cold along the Pacific coast.

Abies concolor

Abies koreana *(detail of cones)*

Other trees will not grow well in the cooler summers because they require hot summers to complete their growth cycle. Factors that can also affect hardiness include exposure to wind (which can dehydrate), winter sun (which can burn foliage and thin bark), and late frosts (which can kill early shoots or flowers).

Foliage Description: These descriptions are meant to provide an overall sense of appearance. Evergreen trees hold their foliage all year long, summer and winter. Deciduous trees lose their leaves in winter. Basic leaf shapes are illustrated on page 16.

Height: Two measurements are separated by a semicolon. The first is "landscape" size: the height most often reached in gardens, parks and yards. The second is "maximum size known": the largest size that this kind of tree has been known to reach either under ideal conditions or with great age. Both of the sizes listed apply only to the species discussed in this book.

Shape and width: See pages 8–9 for an explanation and illustrations of tree shapes.

Characteristics: Describes appearance and features of the trees. Includes information about where the tree is native. "N:" means "native to."

Cultural Information: Explains optimal soil, placement and care.

Abies (A-beez) **fir,** Evergreen foliage ○ ◐ ▉

Zones: Variable

Height: 15 to 70 feet; 100 to 130 feet

Foliage: Short-needled evergreen

Shape: Conical

Characteristics: These magnificent conifers with straight trunks and nearly horizontal branches make impressive specimens in the landscape. Fat, oblong cones are held upright on the branches. The white fir (*Abies concolor;* Zones 3 to 7; N: Rocky Mountains) has attractive blue-green foliage and is one of the most adaptable firs, tolerating more summer heat than most and even doing well in some city conditions. Usually grows to about 50 feet, width is about 25 feet. Nikko fir (*A. homolepsis;* Zones 4 to 6; N: Japan) is a midsize tree that grows to about 50 feet in gardens, often flat topped, with bright green foliage. Korean fir (*A. koreana;* Zones 5 and 6; N: Korea) is a smaller tree with deep green foliage, normally reaching only 30 feet in cultivation, but up to 60 feet in the wild. The immature cones are an attractive purple and may appear even on young trees.

Cultural Information: Firs generally prefer moist, humid conditions and grow best in northern or mountain climates in a well-drained, acid soil. Under these conditions they have few pest and disease troubles. Pruning often destroys their shape. Branches are not regenerated once lost, so avoid crowding by other trees. The foliage of the balsam fir (*A. balsamea;* Zones 3 to 5; N: North America) has a delicate fragrance, but it is the least heat tolerant of firs, dying mysteriously after a few years, except in cool mountainous climates.

Acer (A-ser) **maple,** Fall color, bark, some with colorful twigs in winter ○ ◑ ▙ ◼

Zones: Variable

Height: 15 to 75 feet; 30 to 120 feet

Foliage: Palmately lobed (rarely compound), broad-leaved deciduous

Shape: Globe, some as wide as tall

Characteristics: Maples are one of the most important groups of ornamental trees. Large or small, maples have many desirable attributes, including brilliant fall colors and striking winter bark textures and color. Hedge maple (*Acer campestre*; Zones 4 to 8; N: Europe) resembles Norway maple in appearance with deep green leathery leaves, but normally reaches only about 35 feet. Paperbark maple (*A. griseum*; Zones 4 to 8; N: China) has decorative, peeling cinnamon-colored bark and grows to 30 feet. Its unusual leaves are composed of three leaflets and assume a reddish fall color. The Japanese maple (*A. palmatum*; Zones 5 to 8; N: Asia) is one of the most variable species of trees. Generally, they are medium to small trees, growing to 15 to 25 feet, with brilliant fall color. Some have colored twigs in winter. *A. palmatum* 'Atropurpureum' has deep reddish purple foliage in summer. *A. palmatum* 'Bloodgood' has the deepest red folige and maintains good color all summer. Coral bark maple (*A. palmatum* 'Senkaki' or 'Sangokaku') has twigs that become a striking salmon pink in fall and winter and has golden fall foliage. Members of the *A. palmatum dissectum* group are charac- terized by deeply cut, lacy foliage and a picturesque contorted branching and trunk pattern. They are slow growing with a low, mounded habit when young and include *A. palmatum* 'Crimson Queen' with lacy, burgundy red foliage all summer, and *A. palmatum* 'Ornatum' which is an old cultivar with reddish spring foliage that becomes bronzy light green in summer and fiery orange and yellow in fall. Old specimens may become picturesque specimens more than 12 feet tall.

Amur maple (*A. Ginnala*; Zones 2 to 8; N: China) and Tatarian maple (*A. tataricum*; Zones 3 to 8; N: southeast Europe and western Asia) are small trees with stiff habits, mainly grown for fall color in the North where the Japanese maple is not hardy.

Another group of midsize trees is the striped-bark maple group, which is characterized by interesting green-and-white striped branches and trunks. The moose-wood maple (*A. pensylvanicum*; Zones 3 to 6; N: eastern North America) grows well in mountainous and northern regions with cool summers; it prefers part shade. The red-vein maple (*A. rufinerve*; Zones 5 to 8; N: Japan) is better suited to warmer areas. They both grow about 30 feet high.

Some of the larger-growing maples make excellent shade trees, but they require adequate space, because they can grow to 60 feet or more and nearly as wide. Red maple (*A. rubrum*; Zones 3 to 9) colors to brilliant red and yellow tints in autumn and is native to eastern North America. Perhaps the finest au- tumn foliage display of the larger species is that of sugar maple (*A. saccharum*; Zones 3 to 8). In its native New England, entire mountainsides are lit up with glorious shades of pastel orange and yellow. It grows about half as wide as tall. Norway maple (*A. platanoides*; Zones 3 to 7; N: Europe) is one of the most commonly planted shade trees, with dense, deep green foliage and yellow fall color. It is spreading, often growing as wide as it does tall. *A. platanoides* 'Crimson King' is a popular cultivar with reddish purple foliage all summer. The leaves of *A. platanoides* 'Drummondii' are edged with white. Unfortunately, large maples, particularly Norway maples, tend to have shallow roots that can heave sidewalks and starve lawns and shrubs. Young Norway maples will grow in dense (full) shade and are invading woodlands in some regions, crowding out the native trees.

Cultural Information: Maples generally do best in rich, well-drained soils. A notable exception are the red maples, which will grow in wet soils with poor drainage. Most will grow in partial shade, and the smaller species are often understory species in nature. Striped-bark maples usually do not grow well in sun. All are generally free of serious pest or disease problems.

Acer griseum

Acer saccharum

Acer palmatum '*Atropurpureum*'

Aesculus Hippocastanum

Aesculus Hippocastanum (ES-kew-lus hip-o-kas-TA-num) **horse chestnut,** Flowers, MSP ○ ◑ ▉

Zone: 3 to 8
Height: 60 feet; 100 feet
Foliage: Palmately compound, broad-leaved deciduous
Shape: Globe, nearly as wide as tall
Characteristics: The common horse chestnut, native to Europe, is grown for its spectacular clusters of small white flowers with golden centers. Few large trees can exceed its beauty when in full bloom. It does, however, have drawbacks, the most serious of which is scorched foliage in mid- to late summer due to leaf diseases. Control measures are unnecessary, because the tree is not harmed, but it is unsightly. Horse chestnut is a poor choice for such high-use areas as patios: In spring, the expanding buds drop their sticky resinous coverings all over the ground and the petals fall, and in autumn it sheds large seeds with spiny coverings. *A. H.* 'Baumannii' is a double-flowered, seedless cultivar.
Cultural Information: Easy to grow and adaptable to most soils, if reasonably moist. Forms a tap root, so best transplanted balled-and-burlapped or from containers when young.

Alaska cedar; see *Chamaecyparis*

Albizia Julibrissin (al-BIZ-ee-a ju-lee-BRI-sin) **hardy silk tree, mimosa,** Flowers, LSP–SU ○ ▉

Zones: 6 to 9
Height: 20 to 30 feet; 35 feet

Albizia Julibrissin

Foliage: Lacy, bipinnately compound, broad-leaved deciduous
Shape: Vase, often wider than high
Characteristics: This small tree (native from Iran to China) is popular for its tropical, brushlike pink flowers, feathery foliage and long bloom season, but is limited in hardiness. *A. J.* 'Rosea' and 'E. H. Wilson' are smaller-growing cultivars that can be grown farther north in milder parts of Zone 5. Seeds prolifically, which can cause a big weed problem.
Cultural Information: Adaptable to many soil types and locations. Recently, a serious wilt disease has killed trees in many areas. *A.* 'Charlotte' and *A.* 'Tryon' are reputedly wilt-resistant.

Aleppo pine; see *Pinus*

Amelanchier arborea (am-el-ANG-kee-er ar-BOR-ee-a) **shadbush, serviceberry, service tree, sarvis tree,** Flowers, fruit, fall color, MSP ○ ◑ ▉

Zones: 4 to 9
Height: 20 to 30 feet; 40 feet
Foliage: Simple broad-leaved deciduous
Shape: Upright, rounded, taller than wide
Characteristics: The common name, shadbush, refers to the bloom season, which corresponds to the season in which shad run in the rivers. White flowers are followed by small, edible red fruit in early summer, which attract wildlife. Showy fall colors range from yellow to orange and red. Botanists disagree about the correct names for the different members of *Amelanchier. A. canadensis* and *A. laevis* are similar

Amelanchier arborea

to *A. arborea*. Native to eastern North America.

Cultural Information: Adaptable to many soil types, but grows best in moist soils. Neat in habit and needs little pruning.

American beech; see *Fagus*

American elm; see *Ulmus*

American holly; see *Ilex*

Amur chokecherry; see *Prunus*

Amur maple; see *Acer*

Araucaria araucana (ar-row-KAR-ee-a ar-row-KAN-a) **monkey puzzle tree,** Evergreen foliage ○ ■╚
Zones: 7 to 9
Height: 40 to 60 feet; 90 feet
Foliage: Stiff, flat, spiny, needled evergreen
Shape: Rounded pyramidal
Characteristics: The monkey puzzle tree, native to Chile, is the hardiest species of *Araucaria*. All other species are tropical or subtropical. The foliage of this conifer is deep green and stiff

Araucaria araucana

with a sharp spine on the end of each wide leaflike needle. A unique and coarse form in the landscape.

Cultural Information: Grows best where summers are cool and moist, as in the Pacific Northwest. Has also grown as far north as Wilmington, Delaware, in the East.

Arborvitaes; see *Thuja*

Arizona cypress; see *Cupressus*

Ash; see *Fraxinus*

Ash, European mountain; see *Sorbus*

Ash, green; see *Fraxinus*

Ash, Korean mountain; see *Sorbus*

Ash, mountain; see *Sorbus*

Ash, white; see *Fraxinus*

Austrian pine; see *Pinus*

Bald cypress; see *Taxodium*

Balsam fir; see *Abies*

Beeches; see *Fagus*

Bell, Carolina silver; see *Halesia*

Bell, mountain silver; see *Halesia*

Bell, silver; see *Halesia*

Betula (BET-you-la) **birch,** Fall color, bark ○ ■╚
Zones: Variable
Height: 40 to 70 feet; 80 to 90 feet
Foliage: Simple broad-leaved deciduous

Shape: rounded pyramidal, about ⅔ as wide as tall

Characteristics: Birches are best known for the white peeling bark of the native paper birch. This tree is a poor choice in warm climates, where it is susceptible to borers. The best choice for white trunks in most regions is the Japanese *B. platyphylla japonica* 'White Spire' (Zones 4 to 7). Another fine landscape plant is the native river birch (*Betula nigra* 'Heritage'; Zones 5 to 7). It has beautiful peeling bark of salmon and tan. The yellow fall color is of short duration. Both of these should be planted as single-trunked trees to avoid future snow and ice damage. Gray birch (*B. populifolia*; Zones 3 to 6; N: northeastern North America) is a smaller tree, growing to about 30 feet, with a grayish white bark. It normally forms several weak trunks, is likely to be damaged by snow and ice when older and is subject to serious leaf-miner damage. Resistant to borers, but not a recommended landscape plant.

Cultural Information: Prefers a moist, acid soil, but will grow on drier sites. River birch tolerates poor drainage. Borer is the most serious threat to birches. River birch is one of the most resistant, and *B. platyphylla japonica* 'White Spire' seems to be the most resistant of the white-trunked birches.

Birches; see *Betula*

Bishop pine; see *Pinus*

Black locust, golden; see *Robinia*

Betula platyphylla japonica

Black pine, Japanese; see *Pinus*

Black tupelo; see *Nyssa*

Bloodgood maple; see *Acer*

Blue Atlas cedar; see *Cedrus*

Blue spruce; see *Picea*

Bullbay; see *Magnolia*

California incense cedar; see *Calocedrus*

California live oak; see *Quercus*

Callery pear; see *Pyrus*

Calocedrus decurrens (kal-oh-SED-rus dee-KER-enz) **California incense cedar,** Evergreen foliage ○ ■
Zones: 5 to 8
Height: 40 to 50 feet; 150 feet
Foliage: Scalelike, needled evergreen
Shape: Fastigiate-conical
Characteristics: This stately conifer, native to the mountains of Oregon and California, is similar in appearance to arborvitae. It tends to be more narrow in shape in the East than in the West.
Cultural Information: Grows best in moist, well-drained soil but is also drought tolerant when well established. Grows well in the southeastern states as well as many other regions.

Canadian hemlock; see *Tsuga*

Canary Island pine; see *Pinus*

Canyon live oak; see *Quercus*

Calocedrus decurrens

Carolina silver bell; see *Halesia*

Carpinus Betulus 'Fastigiata' (kar-PI-nus BET-you-lus) **European hornbeam,** Refined shape, foliage ○ ◑ ■
Zones: 4 to 7
Height: 40 to 50 feet; 75 feet
Foliage: Simple broad-leaved deciduous
Shape: Fastigiate, about ⅔ as wide as high
Characteristics: Carpinus Betulus 'Fastigiata' (native to Europe and Asia Minor) is the most noteworthy form of this species. Its rounded upright habit and neat green foliage make a shapely

Carpinus Betulus *'Fastigiata'*

Catalpa bignonioides

specimen tree. Fall color is yellowish green.
Cultural Information: Adaptable to a wide range of soils and requires infrequent pruning.

Catalpa (ka-TAL-pa) **catalpa,** Flowers, ESU ○ ◑ ■
Zones: Variable
Height: 30 to 60 feet; 100 feet
Foliage: Large, simple, heart-shaped, broad-leaved deciduous
Shape: Globe, spread varies
Characteristics: Spectacular summer-flowering trees with large clusters of small bell-shaped white flowers with yellow and purple spots, followed by long

beanlike pods. The large, heart-shaped leaves turn yellowish green in fall. Northern catalpa (*Catalpa speciosa*; Zones 4 to 8) grows 40 to 60 feet tall and about half as wide as high. Common or southern catalpa (*C. bignonioides*; Zones 5 to 9) is small growing, reaching only 30 to 40 feet but forming a tree as wide as tall. Both are native to the southeastern United States. *Cultural Information:* An adaptable species that tolerates hot, dry conditions, but grows best in moist, rich soils.

Cedar; see *Cedrus*

Cedar, Alaska; see *Chamaecyparis*

Cedar, blue Atlas; see *Cedrus*

Cedar, California incense; see *Calocedrus*

Cedar, deodar; see *Cedrus*

Cedar, eastern red; see *Juniperus*

Cedar, Japanese; see *Cryptomeria*

Cedar, Port Orford; see *Chamaecyparis*

Cedar, western red; see *Juniperus*

Cedar, white; see *Thuja*

Cedar of Lebanon; see *Cedrus*

Cedrus (SEE-drus) **cedar,** Evergreen foliage ○ ■
Zones: Variable
Height: 40 to 70 feet; over 100 feet

Foliage: Short-needled evergreen
Shape: Broadly pyramidal, about ⅔ as wide as high
Characteristics: Cedars mature to grand, massive trees with a broader shape than most conifers, so they must be allowed plenty of space in which to grow. Blue Atlas cedar (*Cedrus atlantica* 'Glauca'), popular for its bluish needles, has the most striking foliage color of the true cedars. Native to the Atlas Mountains of northern Africa, hardy in Zones 6 to 9. Deodar cedar (*C. Deodara*; Zones 7 to 9; N: Himalaya) has longer green needles than the other cedars and a soft, graceful appearance in the landscape. *C.* 'Shalimar' is a hardier cultivar, growing in Boston in Zone 6. The famed cedar of Lebanon (*C. libanii*; Zones 5 to 7; N: Asia Minor) is the widest-growing species and has dark green foliage.
Cultural Information: Adaptable to various well-drained soils. Seldom bothered by pests and diseases.

Cercidiphyllum japonicum (ser-si-di-FIL-um ja-PON-i-kum)
katsura tree, Summer foliage, fall color ○ ◑ ■
Zones: 4 to 8
Height: 50 feet; 100 feet
Foliage: Heart-shaped, broad-leaved deciduous
Shape: Globe, about as wide as tall
Characteristics: One of the most beautiful of the nonflowering trees. Its clean, deep green, heart-shaped foliage emerges reddish purple in spring and changes to pastel yellow and apricot-orange in autumn. The freshly fallen leaves have a delightful, spicy fragrance. Native to Japan and China.

Left: Cedrus Deodara
Middle: Cedrus atlantica '*Glauca*'
Bottom: Cercidiphyllum japonicum

Cultural Information: Katsura trees are easy to grow and tolerant of city conditions. They are generally pest and disease free.

Cercis canadensis (SER-sis kan-a-DEN-sis) **eastern redbud**, Flowers, SP ○ ◐ ▙

Zones: 4 to 9

Height: 20 to 30 feet; 30 feet

Foliage: Heart-shaped, broad-leaved deciduous

Shape: Globe-vase, as wide, or wider, than high

Characteristics: Small lavender to purplish pink flowers bloom along branches before leaves in early to midspring. Blooms just before dogwood and evergreen azaleas. Foliage may color to yellow in autumn. *Cercis canadensis* 'Forest Pansy' has purplish foliage all summer. Native to eastern North America.

Cultural Information: Adaptable to a wide range of soil types if they are well drained. Grows well as an understory tree in light shade. Appearance is improved when dead wood is pruned out periodically.

Cercis canadensis 'Forest Pansy'

Chamaecyparis pisifera 'Filifera'

Chain, golden; see ***Laburnum***

Chamaecyparis (kam-ee-SIP-ar-is) **false cypress,** Evergreen foliage, bark ○ ◐ ▙ ▆

Zones: Variable

Height: 50 to 75 feet; more than 150 feet

Foliage: Scalelike needled evergreen

Shape: Pyramidal-conical, ¼ to ⅓ as wide as high

Characteristics: False cypresses are reliable garden conifers that are slightly smaller than firs, true cedars and larger pines. Many have warm reddish brown bark. There are numerous varieties, including many dwarf or slow-growing selections (not discussed in this book). *Chamaecypacis pisifera,* The Sawara false cypress or retinospora (Zones 3 to 8; N: Japan) is probably the most commonly grown species with many different foliage forms and colors. *C. p.* 'Boulevard' has soft plumy blue foliage. It is somewhat untidy as a large tree because dead foliage is held among the branches. Thread-leaf cypress (*C. p.* 'Filifera') has long, stringy branchlets that create a unique foliage texture. It is slow growing and remains a small tree. Golden thread-leaf cypress (*C. p.* 'Filifera Aurea') has stringy golden foliage that colors best in winter. *C. p.* 'Plumosa' has dark green, feathery foliage. Moss cypress (*C. p.* 'Squarrosa') has soft, plumy, light blue-green foliage.

Hinoki false cypress (*C. obtusa*; Zones 4 to 8; N: Japan) is most often seen in its dwarf forms, but the normal form makes a fine tree to 75 feet with lustrous dark green foliage and rich reddish brown bark. *C. o.* 'Crippsii' is an excellent golden-foliaged conifer with somewhat slower growth. There are also many different varieties of Lawson false cypress or Port Orford cedar (*C. Lawsoniana*; Zones 5 to 7; N: Pacific Northwest) but they do not thrive in heat, and are not commonly grown in most of the United States. *C. L.* 'Columnaris' is especially useful for its steely blue foliage and refined, narrow, conical habit. Weeping nootka false cypress or Alaska cedar (*C. nootkatensis* 'Pendula'; Zones 5 to 9; N: Alaska to Oregon) makes a smaller, broadly pyramidal tree with drooping branchlets and deep green foliage. It reaches only about 40 feet in gardens, but more than 100 feet in the wild.

Cultural Information: Most are easy to grow and adapted to a variety of soils if well drained, but prefer soil to be rich and moist. Sawara and Hinoki false cypresses are better suited to warmer, drier climates than the others.

Cherry; see ***Prunus***

Cherry, Cornelian; see ***Cornus***

Cherry, double sweet; see ***Prunus***

Cherry, Higan; see ***Prunus***

Cherry, Japanese flowering; see ***Prunus***

Cherry, Yoshina; see ***Prunus***

Cherry laurel, Portugese; see ***Prunus***

Chestnut, horse; see *Aesculus*

China fir; see *Cunninghamia*

Chinese elm; see *Ulmus*

Chinese fringe tree; see *Chionanthus*

Chinese juniper; see *Juniperus*

Chinese quince; see *Pseudocydonia*

Chionanthus (ky-oh-NAN-thus) **fringe tree,** flowers, LSP. ○ ▋▙
Zones: Variable
Height: 20 feet; 30 feet
Foliage: Simple broad-leaved deciduous
Shape: Spreading, globe, about as wide as high
Characteristics: Small, fragrant flowers in fluffy clusters cover the tree when in full bloom. Leathery foliage is a lustrous dark green, yellow-green in fall. The blue berries ripen in early fall and, although not particularly showy, are attractive to birds. If not trained to have a single trunk, trees may become attractive, large multistemmed shrubs. Usually dioecious, so you'll need both sexes in the same vicinity to produce fruit. *Chionanthus virginicus* is native to the southeastern United States, and hardy in Zones 3 to 9. The Chinese fringe tree (*C. retusus;* Zones 5 to 8; N: Asia) has smaller, lighter green leaves. Both are fine ornamentals.
Cultural Information: Prefers rich, acid, moist soil. Requires little pruning and is seldom attacked by pests and diseases.

Chokecherry, Amur; see *Prunus*

Cladrastis lutea (kla-DRAS-tis lew-TEE-a) **yellowwood,** Flowers, bark, LSP ○ ▋▙
Zones: 3 to 8
Height: 40 feet; 50 feet
Foliage: Pinnately compound, broad-leaved deciduous
Shape: Spreading globe, as wide as high
Characteristics: Pendulous clusters of white pea-like flowers hang from the ends of the branches. Leaves are light green; bark is smooth and gray, much like that of beech. Native to southeastern United States.
Cultural Information: Requires well-drained soil, which may be either acid or alkaline. Prune only in summer to avoid bleeding in winter and spring. Tends to form weak, narrow crotches, which should be spread or corrected by pruning when young.

Coast redwood; see *Sequoia*

Colorado spruce; see *Picea*

Common catalpa; see *Catalpa*

Contorted willow; see *Salix*

Coral bark maple; see *Acer*

Cork oak; see *Quercus*

Cornelian cherry; see *Cornus*

Chionanthus retusus

Cladrastis lutea

Cladrastis lutea
(detail of flowers)

Cornus florida

Cornus Kousa

Cornus (KOR-nus) dogwood,
Flowers, fruit, fall color, bark, SP-ESU ○ ◑ ⬛ ⬛

Zones: Variable
Height: 20 to 30 feet; 40 feet
Foliage: Simple broad-leaved deciduous
Shape: Spreading vase, as wide, or wider, than high
Characteristics: Best known is the showy flowering dogwood (*Cornus florida*; Zones 5 to 9) native to the eastern United States. Its showy "petals" are actually colored leaf bracts that may be white, pink or a deep pink approaching red, depending on the tree. In many of the eastern states, this tree is part of a classic combination, blooming with azaleas in midspring. Many cultivars are available with improved bract color and size. In fall, the foliage colors to reddish purple with clusters of red berries. Kousa dogwood (*C. Kousa*; Zones 5 to 8) is a similar species from Japan and China, but it flowers about a month later, in late spring to early summer. Bracts are usually white; however, rare pink cultivars are now becoming available. Red fall color and edible round red fruits appear in fall. Bark mottled with tan and gray-brown is attractive all year. Cornelian cherry (*C. mas*; Zones 4 to 8; N: Europe) is very different. It does not have bracts, but it does produce many clusters of small yellow flowers in early spring, long before other trees. Combines well with the early small bulbs. Edible red "cherries" may be used for preserves in fall. *C. officinalis* (Zones 5 to 8; N: Japan and Korea) is similar, but flowers a week or so earlier and has more attractive mottled bark.
Cultural Information: Grows best in well-drained, moist, acid soil, under semiwoodland conditions. In recent years, *C. florida* has been afflicted by a debilitating anthracnose disease in many areas. Trees located where there is good air circulation and suitable soil seem to do best. Provide good care, including water in drought periods, to maintain vigor. Trees are seldom killed outright and may remain fine ornamentals if infection is moderate. Dogwood are damaged especially easily by such things as lawn mowers bumping into the trunks. These wounds give entry to borers and diseases that lead to the tree's decline.

Corylus Colurna (KOR-i-lus ko-LUR-na) Turkish filbert, Turkish hazel, Flowers, fall color, ESP ○ ⬛

Zones: 4 to 7
Height: 50 feet; 75 feet
Foliage: Simple broad-leaved deciduous
Shape: Pyramidal, about ½ as wide as tall
Characteristics: An attractive, moderate-size tree, native to southeastern Europe and Asia Minor. Grown for its clean, dark green foliage and stately, low-branching formal shape. Both male and female flowers occur on the same tree, but it is the male flowers that are showy. They are produced in the very early spring in long, hanging greenish catkins. Fall foliage is not striking, but may develop shades of yellow and purple.

Corylus Colurna

Corylus Colurna *(detail of catkins)*

Crataegus viridis *'Winter King'*

Cultural Information: Plant Turkish filberts in well-drained soil. They will withstand more drought than many shade trees, and so are useful for drier sites. Also tolerant of heat and city conditions. Seldom bothered by pests and diseases.

Crabapple; see *Malus*

Crataegus (kra-TEE-gus) **hawthorn,** Flowers, fruit, fall color, MSP ○ ▮

Zones: Variable
Height: 15 to 30 feet; 35 feet
Foliage: Palmately lobed, broad-leaved deciduous
Shape: Globe, as wide as high
Characteristics: Named for the long thorns, characteristic of many species. Most have clusters of white flowers followed by small red fruits in fall. Fall color ranges from yellow and orange to purple tints. The English hawthorn (*Crataegus oxycantha*) is popular for its pink or red flowers, particularly the double red cultivar *C. o.* 'Paul's Scarlet'. But the English hawthorn is very susceptible to leaf-spot disease and lacks fall color

and fruit. It grows to 15 feet. Winter king hawthorn (*C. viridis* 'Winter King'; Zones 5 to 7; N: eastern North America) is one of the best for general landscape use. It has shorter and sparser thorns, a more vaselike tree shape to 30 feet, white flowers and profuse, bright red fruit that lasts through much of the winter.

Cultural Information: Despite various insect and disease problems, hawthorns are easy to grow in a variety of conditions. They will tolerate either acid or alkaline soils as well as drought. Training and regular pruning is necessary to produce a well-shaped tree, because they tend to sucker and develop crossing branches. Pests and diseases may include lace bugs, aphids, borers, scales, mites, scab and fire blight.

Cryptomeria japonica (krip-to-MEE-ri-a ja-PON-i-ka) **Japanese cedar,** Evergreen foliage, bark ○ ◑ ▮

Zones: 6 to 9
Height: 60 feet; 100 feet

Foliage: Prickly scalelike needled evergreen
Shape: Fastigiate-conical, ⅓ to ½ as wide as high
Characteristics: Japanese cedars, native to Japan and China, make handsome specimen conifers throughout the year, with deep green foliage in spring and summer that becomes bronzy in winter. They tend to retain their lower branches. The shredding bark is reddish brown. *Cryptomeria japonica* 'Elegans' has softer, bushier foliage that turns reddish in winter, and it reaches only 10 to 15 feet. *C. j.* 'Lobbii' is a full-size tree, but somewhat sparsely branched, which makes for an open, picturesque effect. *C. j.* 'Sekkan' is slower growing with golden new growth. *C. j.* 'Yoshino' is perhaps the finest cultivar, with a dense branching habit and an evenly shaped tree.

Cultural Information: Grows best in a rich woodland soil that is well drained, light and moist. Few pests and diseases bother Japanese cedars.

Cryptomeria japonica
'Yoshino'

Cunninghamia lanceolata (kun-ing-HAM-i-a lan-see-oh-LAY-ta) China fir, Evergreen foliage ○ ◑ ▦

Zones: 7 to 9

Height: 60 to 75 feet; 150 feet

Foliage: needled evergreen

Shape: Pyramidal, about ⅓ as wide as high

Characteristics: These native Chinese conifers have a unique, almost tropical appearance because of their long, flat needles. Branches tend to be held horizontally, and trees that have been broken may develop more than one trunk. *Cunninghamia lanceolata* 'Glauca' has blue-green foliage.

Cultural Information: Of limited hardiness, this conifer will often grow in the warmer parts of Zone 6. Unfortunately it is susceptible to breakage from strong winds, ice and heavy snow, and most specimens seem to lose their tops at least once. New tops readily form, a trait unusual among conifers, but these should be thinned to a single new leader. Also unusual is the ability to sprout from the base of the trunk. Plant in an acidic, well-drained soil. Usually pest and disease free.

Cunninghamia lanceolata

×Cupressocyparis Leylandii (kew-press-oh-SIP-ar-is lay-LAN-dee-i) Leyland cypress, evergreen foliage. ○ ▦

Zones: 6 to 10

Height: 70 feet; more than 100 feet

Foliage: Scalelike needled evergreen

Shape: Fastigiate to pyramidal, less than ¼ as wide as high

Characteristics: This hybrid conifer (*Cupressus macrocarpa* × *Chamaecyparis nootkatensis*) is rapidly becoming one of the most popular landscape plants where hardy. It is one of the fastest-growing evergreen trees, easily making 3 feet of growth a year under good conditions. There are many cultivars. ×*Cupressocyparis Leylandii* 'Haggerston Grey' has grayish green foliage with a narrow tree shape. *C. L.* 'Leighton Green' has bright green foliage. *C. L.* 'Robinson's Gold' and *C. L.* 'Castlewellan' have yellow foliage in cool climates, but not where summers are hot. The foliage of *C. L.* 'Silver Dust' is attractively flecked with white, making it one of the best large variegated conifers.

Cultural Information: Adapted to a wide range of conditions and well-drained soils. Trees tend to be unstable and topple over in wind, due to small root systems. Plant as young as possible from containers and be sure to spread roots. An excellent screening plant that makes a good hedge if pruned yearly to maintain size. Also good for seashore plantings. No serious pests or diseases.

Cupressus (kew-PRES-sis) cypress, Evergreen foliage ○ ▦

Zones: Variable

Height: 30 to 40 feet; 75 feet

Foliage: Scalelike needled evergreen

Shape: Fastigiate to pyramidal, ½ as wide as high

Characteristics: These true cypresses are conifers for the South, rather than for cold climates. Perhaps the most famous to Americans is the Monterey cypress (*Cupressus macrocarpa*; Zones 8 to 10) of coastal California. It forms a widely fastigiate to pyramidal tree that broadens out with age to reveal a picturesque form. Arizona cypress (*C. arizonica*; Zones 6 to 9) is a hardier but smaller tree growing to 35 feet with bluish gray

×Cupressocyparis Leylandii

Cupressus macrocarpa

Cunninghamia lanceolata *(detail of cones)*

Cupressus arizonica
and C. macrocarpa

foliage. Italian cypress *(C. sempervirens*; Zones 7 to 10) is the narrow, spiky tree seen in classical landscapes of Italy. In the United States, it grows best in the similar climate of coastal California.

Cultural Information: Cypresses are easy to grow because established trees are quite drought resistant, need little pruning unless used as a hedge, and are pest and disease resistant. Arizona and Monterey cypresses are subject to canker diseases. Plant in a well-drained soil.

Cypress; see *Cupressus*

Cypress, Arizona; see ***Cupressus***

Cypress, bald; see ***Taxodium***

Cypress, false; see ***Chamaecyparis***

Cypress, golden thread-leaf; see ***Chamaecyparis***

Cypress, Hinoki false; see ***Chamaecyparis***

Cypress, Italian; see ***Cupressus***

Cypress, Lawson false; see ***Chamaecyparis***

Cypress, Leyland; see × ***Cupressocyparis***

Cypress, Monterey; see ***Cupressus***

Cypress, moss; see ***Chamaecyparis***

Cypress, Sawara false; see ***Chamaecyparis***

Cypress, thread-leaf; see ***Chamaecyparis***

Cypress, weeping nootka false; see ***Chamaecyparis***

Davidia involucrata (day-VID-i-a in-vol-u-KRAY-ta) **dove tree, handkerchief tree,** Flowers, bark, MSP ○ ◑ ■
Zones: 6 to 8
Height: 20 to 40 feet; 65 feet
Foliage: Simple broad-leaved deciduous
Shape: Spreading pyramidal, usually narrower than tall
Characteristics: The common names of this Chinese native are suggested by the large white bracts (petallike leaves) that hang below the branches when the tree is in bloom. The shiny, dark green leaves are attractive all summer, but do not color in autumn. The scaly bark is showy all year with warm shades of brown and orange-brown. Young trees are slow to reach flowering age.
Cultural Information: This Chinese woodlander prefers light shade, but will tolerate full sun if not drought stressed. Soil should be rich, moist and well drained.

Davidia involucrata

Dawn redwood; see **Meta-sequoia**

Deodar cedar; see **Cedrus**

Dogwoods; see **Cornus**

Double sweet cherry; see **Prunus**

Douglas fir; see **Pseudotsuga**

Dove tree; see **Davidia**

Dragon's claw willow; see **Salix**

Eastern arborvitae; see **Thuja**

Eastern redbud; see **Cercis**

Eastern red cedar; see **Juniperus**

Eastern white pine; see **Pinus**

Elms; see **Ulmus**

English hawthorn; see **Crataegus**

English holly; see **Ilex**

English oak, Fastigiate; see **Quercus**

European beech; see **Fagus**

European hornbeam; see **Carpinus**

European larch; see **Larix**

European mountain ash; see **Sorbus**

Fagus (FAY-gus) **beech,** Bark, foliage ○ ◑ ■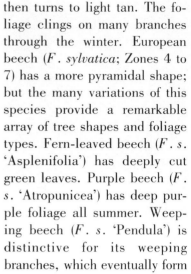
Zones: Variable
Height: 50 to 70 feet, more than 100 feet
Foliage: Simple broad-leaved deciduous
Shape: Globe or pyramidal, about ⅔ as wide as high
Characteristics: Beeches are well known for their smooth, light gray trunks. The American beech (*Fagus grandifolia*; Zones 3 to 9) forms a fine rounded shade tree with green foliage that becomes golden yellow in autumn,

then turns to light tan. The foliage clings on many branches through the winter. European beech (*F. sylvatica*; Zones 4 to 7) has a more pyramidal shape; but the many variations of this species provide a remarkable array of tree shapes and foliage types. Fern-leaved beech (*F. s.* 'Asplenifolia') has deeply cut green leaves. Purple beech (*F. s.* 'Atropunicea') has deep purple foliage all summer. Weeping beech (*F. s.* 'Pendula') is distinctive for its weeping branches, which eventually form

Fagus sylvatica *'Asplenifolia'*

Fagus sylvatica *'Pendula'*

a large mound shape. All beeches need plenty of space in order to grow into grand specimens.

Cultural Information: Plant in a well-drained, preferably acid soil. Transplant in spring. Tolerant of shade, but grows best in full sun. Not good under city conditions. The shallow roots compete with underplantings.

False cypresses; see ***Chamaecyparis***

Fastigiate English oak; see ***Quercus***

Fern-leaved beech; see ***Fagus***

Filbert, Turkish; see ***Corylus***

Fir; see ***Abies***

Fir, balsam; see ***Abies***

Fir, China; see ***Cunninghamia***

Fir, Douglas; see ***Pseudotsuga***

Fir, Korean; see ***Abies***

Fir, Nikko; see ***Abies***

Fir, white; see ***Abies***

Flowering cherry, Japanese; see ***Prunus***

Flowering dogwood; see ***Cornus***

Foster holly; see ***Ilex***

Fragrant snowbell; see ***Styrax***

Franklin tree; see ***Franklinia***

Franklinia Alatamaha

(frank-LIN-i-a a-la-ta-MA-ha) **Franklin tree,** Flowers, fall color, LSU-EF ○ ◑ ▙

Zones: 5 to 9

Height: 15 to 20 feet; 30 feet

Foliage: Simple broad-leaved deciduous

Shape: Spreading globe, often nearly as wide as high

Characteristics: This beautiful, small tree has not been seen in the wild since discovered and collected in Georgia by Philadelphia botanist John Bartram, in the late 1700s. He named it after his friend Benjamin Franklin. It is one of the finest small flowering trees or large shrubs, often forming several trunks. White camellialike flowers with yellow stamens are borne for more than a month extending into autumn, when they combine with reddish foliage. The growth habit is rounded and spreading, but open so that larger specimens combine well with underplantings.

Cultural Information: Grows best in a rich, acid, well-drained, moist soil, such as along a stream bank, but performs well in many garden situations. Flowers most prolifically in full sun. Easiest to transplant when small.

Fraxinus (FRAK-si-nus) **ash,** Foliage, fall color ○ ▙

Zones: 3 to 9

Height: 50 to 80 feet; more than 100 feet

Foliage: Pinnately compound broad-leaved deciduous

Shape: Globe

Characteristics: Ashes are useful shade trees because of their

Franklinia Alatamaha

Fraxinus pennsylvanica 'Summit'

rapid growth and their adaptability to a variety of sites and soils where other trees may not perform well. Leaves are composed of several leaflets and are coarse in texture. Some ashes produce abundant seeds that may lead to a weed problem, so male cultivars, which are seedless, are recommended. Green ash (*Fraxinus pennsylvanica*) is the most adaptable and transplants readily, but often lacks fall color. *F. p.* 'Marshall's Seedless' and *F. p.* 'Patmore' are seedless. White ash (*F. americana*), although less adaptable,

is entirely suitable for most home garden conditions and has superior ornamental value. Fall color ranges from yellow to purple. *F. a.* 'Autumn Purple' is seedless. Both species are native to eastern North America.
Cultural Information: Adaptable to both acid and alkaline soils, and green ash tolerates drier sites and salt. Easily transplanted. May be attacked by numerous pests and diseases, but these are usually not severe, because trees tend to maintain their health under adverse conditions. Prune in fall.

Fringe trees; see ***Chionanthus***

Giant redwood; see ***Sequoiadendron***

Ginkgo biloba (GINK-go by-LOW-ba) **maidenhair tree,** Foliage, fall color ○ ◼️⌐
Zones: 3 to 9
Height: 80 feet; more than 100 feet
Foliage: Fan-shaped broad-leaved deciduous
Shape: Fastigiate to spreading globe, usually narrower than wide.
Characteristics: Ginkgos have been cultivated in China for centuries and have even been found in fossils. The leaves, shaped like little fans, are bright green in summer and golden yellow in fall. The seeds ripen in fall and have a fleshy covering, which ferments to a strong putrid odor. Because ginkos are dioecious, you can prevent the formation of fruit by planting only male trees. *Ginkgo biloba* 'Sentry' is a fastigiate male cultivar.

Ginkgo biloba

Gleditsia triacanthos
'Sunburst'

Cultural Information: Adapted to wide range of soil conditions, tolerant of air pollution and city conditions, and mostly pest and disease free.

Gleditsia triacanthos (gle-DIT-see-a try-a-KAN-thos) **honey locust,** Foliage, fall color ○ ◼️⌐
Zones: 3 to 9
Height: 70 feet; more than 100 feet
Foliage: Lacy pinnately or bipinnately compound, broad-leaved, deciduous
Shape: Spreading vase, often about as wide as high
Characteristics: The leaves are composed of many small leaflets that cast a light shade. In autumn, these leaflets fall individually, and are small enough virtually to eliminate the need for raking. Fall color of these trees, native to eastern North America, is yellow. Typical honey locusts have long, sharp thorns along the trunk and branches, so only selections of the thornless variety (*Gleditsia triacanthos*

inermis) are planted in gardens. The young foliage of *G. t.* 'Sunburst' is golden yellow, eventually fading to green. *G. t.* 'Ruby Lace' has reddish foliage, but is inferior in habit and pest resistance to other types. Many thornless cultivars with green foliage, including *G. t.* 'Moraine', are available in nurseries.
Cultural Information: Adaptable to a wide range of soils, but seems to prefer those that are moist, rich, and alkaline. Also tolerant of salt and drought. A very popular tree in recent years, but is subject to a number of pests and diseases, including webworm, that may become serious. Seems to do especially well in cities where leaf litter (in which webworm overwinters) is usually cleaned up.

Golden black locust; see ***Robinia***

Golden chain; see ***Laburnum***

Golden larch; see ***Pseudolarix Kaempferi***

Goldenrain tree; see ***Koelreuteria***

Golden thread-leaf cypress; see ***Chamaecyparis***

Golden weeping willow; see ***Salix***

Gray birch; see ***Betula***

Green ash; see ***Fraxinus***

Gum, sour; see ***Nyssa***

Gum, sweet; see ***Liquidambar***

Halesia (ha-LEE-zi-a) **silver bell,** Flowers, fall color, MSP ◑ ○ ◾▪

Zones: Variable

Height: 40 to 60 feet; 60 to 80 feet

Foliage: Simple broad-leaved deciduous

Shape: Pyramidal globe, about ⅔ as wide as high

Characteristics: Silver bells are among the best native ornamental trees; they are native to southeastern North America. The small white flowers hang below the branches. Fall color is yellow or greenish yellow. The Carolina silver bell (*Halesia carolina;* Zones 4 to 8) reaches about 40 feet in normal situations. The mountain silver bell (*H. monticola;* Zones 5 to 8) grows to about 60 feet and has larger flowers. There are pink-flowered forms of both species.

Cultural Information: Grows best in rich, moist, acid soil as an understory tree in light shade, but will take full sun. Few pest or disease problems.

Handkerchief tree; see ***Davidia***

Hardy silk tree; see ***Albizia***

Hawthorns; see ***Crataegus***

Hazel, Turkish; see ***Corylus***

Hedge maple; see ***Acer***

Hemlocks; see ***Tsuga***

Higan cherry; see ***Prunus***

Himalayan pine; see ***Pinus***

Hinoki false cypress; see ***Chamaecyparis***

Hollies; see ***Ilex***

Holly oak; see ***Quercus***

Hollywood juniper; see ***Juniperus***

Holm oak; see ***Quercus***

Honey locust; see ***Gleditsia***

Hornbeam, European; see ***Carpinus***

Horse chestnut; see ***Aesculus***

Idesia polycarpa (eye-DEE-zee-a poly-KAR-pa) **idesia,** Flowers, fruit, LSP-ESU ○ ◑ ◾▪

Zones: 6 to 8

Height: 40 to 60 feet; 60 feet

Foliage: Simple broad-leaved deciduous

Shape: Pyramidal globe, as wide as tall

Characteristics: This rarely seen, but attractive, tree is native to Japan and China. It has large, deep green, heart-shaped leaves and clusters of reddish orange fruit in autumn. The clusters of greenish flowers are not especially showy.

Cultural Information: Plant in a moist, well-drained soil. Idesias are dioecious, so both sexes must be present in order for fruit to be produced.

Ilex (EYE-lex) **holly,** Fruit, evergreen foliage, SP ○ ◑ ◾▪

Zones: Variable

Height: 30 feet; 50 feet or more

Foliage: Simple broad-leaved evergreen

Shape: Pyramidal, about ⅓ as wide as tall

Characteristics: Red berries among spiny evergreen foliage on shapely trees make holly one of the showiest ornamentals of late fall and winter. Most kinds also have yellow-berried varieties, especially pleasant when combined with the red-berried types. American holly (*Ilex opaca;* Zones 5 to 9) is the best species for eastern North America, where it is native. It is the hardiest broad-leaved evergreen tree in the North. The foliage is an olive green. *I. o.* 'Stewarts Silver Crown', a female, is the first American holly to have foliage variegated with cream. Foster holly (*I. × attenuata* 'Foster #2'; Zones 7 to 9) bears abundant crops of berries and has smaller leaves that are easier to use in cut arrangements. English holly (*I. Aquifolium;* Zones 6 to 9) is the finest-looking ornamental holly with deep green glossy foliage and bright red berries. It resents excessive heat

Halesia carolina

Idesia polycarpa

Ilex Aquifolium
'Golden King'

and grows best in the Pacific Northwest, although it does reasonably well in the Mid-Atlantic region. There are also forms with leaves variegated with white or cream. Native to Europe, North Africa and western Asia. *I.* 'Nellie Stevens' (Zones 6 to 9) is a popular hybrid of English holly that does well in the Southeast. Long-stalk holly (*I. pedunculosa*; Zones 5 to 8) is native to Japan and China. It has friendly, spineless, dark green, glossy leaves and bright red berries on long peduncles (fruit stems). It often grows with multiple trunks, but can be trained to a fine single-trunked tree. Normally about 15 feet tall, but may reach 30 feet. Some hollies are deciduous, but those are usually shrubs, and not discussed in this book.

Cultural Information: Hollies grow best in a moist, well-drained, acid soil and will be more densely branched in full sun. American holly is often afflicted with leaf miner, but trees in partial shade and woodland conditions seem less bothered by this. Because they are

dioecious, both sexes must be planted for fruit production. Similar species can pollinate each other if they bloom at the same time.

Incense cedar, California; see *Calocedrus*

Italian cypress; see *Cupressus*

Italian stone pine; see *Pinus*

Japanese birch; see *Betula*

Japanese black pine; see *Pinus*

Japanese cedar; see *Cryptomeria*

Japanese flowering cherry; see *Prunus*

Japanese larch; see *Larix*

Japanese maple; see *Acer*

Japanese pagoda tree; see *Sophora*

Japanese snowbell; see *Styrax*

Japanese stewartia; see *Stewartia*

Japanese umbrella pine; see *Sciadopitys*

Japanese zelkova; see *Zelkova*

Junipers; see *Juniperus*

Juniperus (jew-NIP-er-us) **juniper,** Evergreen foliage ○ ■
Zones: 3 to 9
Height: 20 to 50 feet; 30 to 90 feet
Foliage: Scalelike needled evergreen
Shape: Fastigiate to pyramidal, less than ⅓ as wide as high
Characteristics: Junipers are workhorses of modern landscapes because they are tolerant of so many adverse conditions. They are extremely variable, with the same species encompassing both shrubby and upright tree forms. Foliage is fine textured and may be prickly, especially on young trees. Foliage color varies from deep green to a grayish blue, depending on the variety. Most common of the tree types is the Chinese juniper (*Juniperus chinensis*), native to Asia. One of the most popular cultivars of this species is *J. c.* 'Kiazuka', also known as 'Torulosa' and Hollywood juniper. It has an irregular branching habit with bright green foliage; it grows to about 25 feet. *J. c.* 'Mountbatten' has a narrow columnar shape and gray-green foliage, and seldom exceeds 12 feet. Western red cedar (*J. scopulorum*; N: western North America) usually grows to about 35 feet and is best known for *J. s.* 'Skyrocket', a strongly narrow, upright cultivar. *J. s.* 'Tolleson's Weeping' has bluish pendulous foliage hanging from weeping branches. Eastern red cedar (*J. virginiana*; N: eastern and central North America) is similar to the western red cedar, but somewhat taller, often reaching 40 to 50 feet. Cultivars include *J. v.* 'Cupressifolia' with dark

Juniperus scopulorum 'Tolleson's Weeping' (detail)

Juniperus chinensis 'Hetzii Columnaris'

green foliage and *J. v.* 'Manhattan Blue', both with a pyramidal habit.

Cultural Information: Generally a tough group of plants. Adaptable to a wide range of soils, including poor, dry, gravelly, acid and alkaline. They prefer an open, sunny location with good air circulation.

Katsura tree; see *Cercidiphyllum*

Koelreuteria paniculata (kol-roo-TE-ri-a pan-ik-you-LAY-ta) **goldenrain tree,** Flowers, fruit, ESU-MSU ○ ◼
Zones: 5 to 9
Height: 30 to 40 feet; 60 feet
Foliage: Pinnate or bipinnately compound, broad-leaved deciduous
Shape: Globe, as wide or wider than high
Characteristics: Small yellow flowers in large clusters among large leaves composed of many smaller leaflets. Large clusters of papery seedpods remain through the winter and are useful in dried arrangements. Native to Asia.
Cultural Information: Adaptable to a wide range of acid and alkaline soils. Tolerates heat, drought and city conditions. Usually not bothered by pests and diseases. Prune to remove crowded or crossing branches in winter.

Korean fir; see *Abies*

Korean mountain ash; see *Sorbus*

Korean pine; see *Pinus*

Korean stewartia; see *Stewartia*

Kousa dogwood; see *Cornus*

Laburnum ×Watereri (la-BER-num wa-TER-er-i) **golden chain,** Flowers, MSP ◑ ◼
Zones: 5 to 7
Height: 15 feet; 30 feet
Foliage: Trifoliate broad-leaved deciduous
Shape: Vase, nearly as wide as tall
Characteristics: A small tree, popular for its hanging clusters of yellow flowers. Beanlike pods in fall are not particularly decorative.
Cultural Information: Grows best in cool regions such as the Pacific Northwest; not suitable for the southeastern United States. Young trees perform well in the East, but decline when they reach middle age. Adapted to well-drained acid or alkaline soils. Locate where they will receive shade during midday.

Lacebark elm; see *Ulmus*

Lacebark pine; see *Pinus*

Larch; see *Larix*

Larch, European; see *Larix*

Larch, golden; see *Pseudolarix*

Larch, Japanese; see *Larix*

Larix (LAR-iks) **larch,** Foliage, fall color ○ ◼
Zones: Variable
Height: 70 to 90 feet, more than 100 feet
Foliage: Short-needled deciduous
Shape: Pyramidal, about ⅓ as wide as high
Characteristics: The needles of this deciduous conifer are bright

Koelreuteria paniculata

Laburnum × Watereri

green and turn yellow in fall. Larches are northern trees. They are not suitable for the southeastern United States because they dislike summer heat. They have a fast rate of growth. Japanese larch (*Larix Kaempferi* or *L. leptolepis*; Zones 4 to 7; N: Japan) is considered a better ornamental, is more disease resistant and is faster growing than the European larch. European larch (*L. decidua*; Zones 2 to 6; N: Europe) is similar in appearance and hardier.
Cultural Information: Plant in acid soil, avoid droughty locations. Transplant when dormant. Prune in summer.

Larix decidua

Laurel; Portuguese cherry; see ***Prunus***

Lawson false cypress; see ***Chamaecyparis***

Lebanon, cedar of; see ***Cedrus***

Leyland cypress; see ×***Cupressocyparis***

Linden, small-leaved; see ***Tilia***

Top left: Liquidambar Styraciflua *Top right:* Liriodendron Tulipifera 'Aureo-marginatum' *Bottom:* Liriodendron Tulipifera *(detail of flower)*

Liquidambar Styraciflua (lik-wid-AM-bar sty-ra-se-FLOO-a) **sweet gum,** Fall color, summer foliage ○ ■▦
Zones: 5 to 9

Height: 60 to 75 feet; more than 100 feet
Foliage: Palmately lobed broad-leaved deciduous
Shape: Pyramidal, about ⅔ as wide as tall
Characteristics: One of the best trees for brilliant autumn colors of yellow to purplish red. The deep green foliage is somewhat star-shaped, with five pointed lobes. The spherical fruit can be a nuisance in fall and winter, especialy on walkways. *Liquidambar Styraciflua* 'Moraine' is considered the hardiest cultivar. *L. S.* 'Obtusiloba' has rounded leaf lobes and does not produce fruit. Native to eastern North America and Mexico.
Cultural Information: Requires a deep, moist, acid soil to grow best. Not tolerant of city conditions, pollution or drought, but is adapted to both the eastern and western regions of the United States. Transplant only in spring. Prune during winter.

Liriodendron Tulipifera (lir-ee-oh-DEN-dron tew-li-PIF-er-a) **tulip tree, tulip poplar,** Flowers, fall color, LSP ○ ◐ ■▦
Zones: 5 to 9
Height: 70 to 90 feet, more than 150 feet
Foliage: Palmately lobed broad-leaved deciduous
Shape: Pyramidal, rounded with age, ½ as wide as tall
Characteristics: Native to eastern United States, tulip trees are tall and stately with long trunks and an open, branching habit. The bright green foliage turns yellow in autumn and has a distinctly flat-ended shape. The orange and green flowers, similar in shape to tulips, are

interesting, but not particularly showy because they are often high in the tree and blend with the foliage. *Liriodendron Tulipifera* 'Aureo-marginatum' has very attractive yellow-edged leaves. They do not seem to burn as easily as leaves on some variegated trees. *L. T.* 'Fastigiatum' is tall and narrow in habit.
Cultural Information: Requires a rich, acid, well-drained soil. Not tolerant of soil compaction or city conditions. Difficult to transplant except when small because roots are thick, fleshy and widely spaced. Often subject to aphid attack in spring with resulting honeydew deposited on surfaces below. Healthy trees are not harmed and spraying is unnecessary.

Live oaks; see ***Quercus***

Loblolly pine; see ***Pinus***

Locust, golden black; see ***Robinia***

Locust, honey; see ***Gleditsia***

Loebner magnolia; see ***Magnolia***

Lombardy poplar; see ***Populus***

London plane tree; see ***Platanus***

Long-stalk holly; see ***Ilex***

Magnolia (mag-NOH-lee-a)

magnolia, Flowers, fruit, evergreen foliage (sometimes), SP, SU ○ ◑ ◼

Zones: Variable
Height: 20 to 60 feet; 90 feet
Foliage: Simple broad-leaved deciduous or evergreen
Shape: Spreading globe or pyramidal, often as wide as high
Characteristics: Magnolias are an important and varied group of flowering trees. Most are spring blooming and deciduous, and many have a light, delicate fragrance. Swamp magnolia has a strong, sweet fragrance and southern magnolia has a deliciously lemony fragrance. Fruits are conelike pods that split open to reveal fleshy pink or red seeds. These seeds may drop out and hang briefly from threads. "Cones" may ripen to pink or red, depending on the variety, and can be quite striking.

The following deciduous magnolias all bloom in early spring. 'Betty' (Zones 3 to 8) is a hybrid that grows to 10 feet and has reddish purple blooms. 'Galaxy' (Zones 6 to 8), also a hybrid, reaches 20 feet and has deep pink blooms. Loebner magnolia (*M.* ×*Loebneri*; Zones 3 to 8) has white or pink blooms and grows to 30 feet. Saucer magnolia (*M.* ×*Soulangiana*; Zones 4 to 9) also grows to 30 feet, with pink or white blooms. And star magnolia (*M. stellata*; Zones 3 to 8) reaches 20 feet and has white or pink blooms. The semievergreen swamp magnolia (*M. virginiana*; Zones 5 to 9) blooms in white in late spring.

Southern magnolia or bullbay (*M. grandiflora*; Zones 6 to 9) is one of the finest ornamental trees native to North America and it is now grown throughout the world, wherever it is most hardy. Few trees can match its beauty at every season. It has lustrous evergreen foliage, often with the added richness of felty brown hairs, called indumentum, on the underside. Large creamy white, lemon-scented flowers are normally borne for about 6 weeks during late spring or early summer, but some varieties will flower continuously into fall. The best trees develop large showy cones that ripen to bright red in autumn. Unfortunately, the large leaves predispose southern magnolias to damage from heavy snow and ice in winter. It is one of the largest of flowering trees, with some individuals in the wild reaching 90 feet. There is so much variation among the different cultivars that they should be carefully chosen to fit your specific needs. *M. g.* 'Bracken's Brown Beauty' (Zones 7 to 9) is an especially fine foliage plant for its heavy, rusty brown indumentum. Compact habit and smaller leaves add to its beauty. Flowers are in scale at 5 to 6 inches in diameter. Grows to about 30 feet. *M. g.* 'Edith Bogue' (Zones 6 to 9) was awarded the Pennsylvania Horticultural Society's Gold Medal Award for its superior cold hardiness. Narrow, deep green leaves with light indumentum. Flowers are 9 to 12 inches wide with strong fragrance from late spring to early summer. The cones are a reddish color and of moderate size. Upright shape resists snow and ice damage. Maximum size in the North is about 35 feet. *M. g.* 'Glen St. Mary' or 'St. Mary'

Magnolia stellata

Magnolia ×Soulangiana *'Alexandrina' (detail of flower)*

Magnolia grandiflora *(detail of flower)*

(Zones 7 to 9) is one of the most widely sold cultivars. It has fine foliage backed by good indumentum and a smaller, more compact habit than the most vigorous kinds. Noteworthy for flowering at a younger age. Grows to about 20 feet tall. *M. g.* 'Hasse' (Zones 7 to 9) is of upright, compact, narrow habit with dark green foliage and good indumentum. Moderate vigor and size. *M. g.* 'Little Gem' (Zones 7 to 9) is a popular cultivar due to its small size (10 to 20 feet tall). Leaves and flowers are less than half that of other cultivars. Blooms spring and fall, and begins blooming at a very young age. *M. g.* 'Samuel Sommer' (Zones 7 to 9) is an upright, wide-spreading tree with some of the largest of all flowers, up to 14 inches across. Good indumentum. Grows 40 feet tall and almost as wide. *M. g.* 'Timeless Beauty' (Zones 6 to 9) is a new variety with upright habit, flowering continuously through the summer. It is a hybrid with *M. virginiana*. *M.* 'Victoria' (Zones 7 to 9) is considered the hardiest cultivar in the Pacific Northwest. Rusty brown indumentum. Grows to 20 feet tall, about ⅔ as wide.
Cultural Information: Magnolias require rich, acid, well-drained, but not droughty soil. The swamp magnolia will grow in wet, poorly drained soils as well as drier locations. Because magnolias have thick, fleshy roots, they should be transplanted when young from containers or balled-and-burlapped, not bareroot. Magnolias are woodlanders and like the shelter of nearby trees, as long as they are not crowded. They are seldom seriously trou-

Malus floribunda

Malus *'Donald Wyman' (detail of fruit)*

bled by pests and diseases, although scale can be a problem. The flowers of early blooming varieties may be damaged by frosts, especially when planted in southern exposures that encourage the flowers to open even earlier. Southern magnolia is subject to winter foliage damage in the North and should be sited in locations sheltered from wind and extreme cold. *M. grandiflora* 'Edith Bogue' is probably the most cold-tolerant cultivar of southern magnolia currently available.

Magnolia, southern; see *Magnolia*

Maidenhair tree; see *Ginkgo*

Malus (MAY-lus) **crabapple,**
Flowers, fruit, fall color, MSP ○
▪▙

Zones: Variable
Height: 12 to 20 feet; 40 feet
Foliage: Simple broad-leaved deciduous
Shape: Weeping, spreading, or globe, often wider than high
Characteristics: Crabapples are one of the most important groups of flowering trees for northern climates because of their extreme hardiness. Depending on the species, they are native to North America, Japan and China. There are so many kinds that they offer a range of characteristics unequaled by most other trees. In spring, before the leaves have expanded fully, the branches are covered with pink,

red and white flowers. These are often followed by a crop of small red, yellow or amber fruit that may hang on the tree into winter or spring, providing food for wildlife. Fruit of some varieties makes excellent jelly. Young foliage may be tinted red in spring and color again in fall. Some varieties maintain reddish foliage through the summer. Most types have a broad, rounded shape, but some are more upright and spreading, while a few have a weeping habit. Choose the combination of characteristics that suits your needs.

Dr. Thomas L. Green, research plant pathologist at the Morton Arboretum in Lisle, Illinois, has been evaluating crabapples for many years and considers the following varieties to be among the best for general landscape use. All are hybrids and grow to about 20 feet, unless noted. *Malus* 'Adams' (Zones 4 to 8) becomes a rounded tree with red flowers. The red fruit remains attractive on the tree from fall to spring. Reddish young foliage enhances the flowers before turning green for the summer. *M.* 'Bob White' (Zones 5 to 8) has a broad, spreading tree habit with small, light green leaves and white flowers. Attractive yellow fruit ripens in fall and often stays on the tree until spring. *M.* 'Donald Wyman' (Zones 4 to 8) grows into a rounded tree. The white flowers are followed by red fruit in fall that lasts well through winter. *M. floribunda* (Zones 4 to 8; N: Japan) is considered one of the finest species of crabapple with pink buds that open to white flowers. It is a graceful tree with a spreading

habit. The amber fruit is showy throughout autumn. *M.* 'Indian Magic' (Zones 4 to 8) has pink flowers and dark green foliage. Orange-red fruit lasts from fall to spring. The tree has an upright, spreading habit. *M.* 'Jewelberry' (Zones 5 to 8) is perhaps the best dwarf (almost shrubby) cultivar. It may grow to about 12 feet tall and 15 feet wide but is usually seen half as large. White flowers are followed by red fruit that persist until December. *M.* 'Orminston Roy' (Zones 4 to 8) is another fine upright, spreading tree. It bears white flowers and amber fruit that lasts until spring. *M.* 'Prairifire' (Zones 4 to 8) has red flowers complemented by purplish foliage that becomes dark green during the summer. The red fruit holds well until spring. This tree has an upright, spreading habit. *M.* 'Professor Sprenger' (Zones 4 to 8) has white flowers, persistent orange-red fruit and an upright, spreading tree shape. *M.* 'Profusion' (Zones 4 to 8) has purple-bronze foliage through summer and red flowers in spring. The maroon fruit holds well through winter. This rounded tree reaches 25 feet. *M.* 'Sugar Tyme' (Zones 5 to 8) is an upright, spreading tree growing to only about 18 feet. White flowers and red fruit are enhanced by dark green foliage. The fruit persists until spring. *M.* 'White Cascade' (Zones 4 to 8) is a weeping crabapple, growing to 15 feet tall, with fine textured green foliage and white flowers. The amber fruit does not persist well through winter. *Cultural Information:* Plant in a well-drained, acid to slightly alkaline soil. Moderately drought

resistant. Bareroot trees are easy to transplant when dormant, or plant container-grown and balled-and-burlapped stock when in growth. Crabapples need pruning from the start to train them to a desirable shape. Always prune as lightly as possible to avoid stimulating water sprouts and suckers. During winter, prune out undesirable suckers and branches. Most crabapples are grafted, and any suckers from below the graft and from the roots should be removed. Crabapples are attacked by many diseases, including scab, fire blight, cedar-apple rust and powdery mildew. Extremely susceptible varieties can be eyesores for much of the summer. Their desirability as ornamentals depends on their ability to resist infection. Spraying with fungicides is unnecessary if resistant varieties are planted. Few are highly resistant to every disease, but those varieties with mild susceptibility still make acceptable landscape trees.

Maples; see ***Acer***

Metasequoia glyptostroboides (met-a-se-KWOY-a glip-tow-strow-BOY-deez) **dawn redwood,** Foliage, fall color, bark ○■◣

Zones: 4 to 8
Height: 70 feet; more than 100 feet
Foliage: Short-needled deciduous
Shape: Sharply conical, about ⅓ as wide as high
Characteristics: One of the few deciduous conifers. Similar to bald cypress, but grows into a broader, more pointed tree. Foliage is soft and feathery, with the short needles arranged along

Metasequoia glyptostroboides

Monterey cypress; see *Cupressus*

Moosewood maple; see *Acer*

Moss cypress; see *Chamaecyparis*

Mountain ashes; see *Sorbus*

Mountain silver bell; see *Halesia*

Nikko fir; see *Abies*

Nootka false cypress, weeping; see *Chamaecyparis*

Northern catalpa; see *Catalpa*

Norway maple; see *Acer*

Norway spruce; see *Picea*

Nyssa sylvatica (NIS-a sil-VAT-i-ka) **sour gum, black tupelo,** Fall color, foliage ○ ◑ ■.

Zones: 3 to 9

Height: 40 to 50 feet; over 100 feet

Foliage: Simple broad-leaved deciduous

Shape: Pyramidal to rounded with age

Characteristics: One of the most spectacular native trees (eastern United States) for fall colors of bright orange, red and yellow. It is one of the first trees to show fall color, often on a few branches in late summer. Foliage is deep green in summer.

Cultural Information: Prefers a deep, moist soil but is adaptable to a wide range of soils including poorly drained and dry, if they are acid. Not tolerant of city conditions. Difficult to transplant due to long, spreading roots. Plant young container-grown specimens. Pests and diseases are not serious.

Oaks; see *Quercus*

short deciduous twigs. Summer foliage color is light green, becoming rusty orange-brown in fall. Dawn redwood is one of the fastest-growing conifers, often exceeding 3 feet in one year. Found in fossils from fifty million years ago, it was discovered growing in western China in 1941.

Cultural Information: A very adaptable tree that grows well in both the North and South. Does best in a rich, deep, moist, acid, well-drained soil. Easy to transplant and needs almost no pruning. Pest and disease free.

Mimosa; see *Albizia*

Monkey puzzle tree; see *Araucaria*

Nyssa sylvatica

Oxydendrum arboreum *(detail of seed capsules)*

Oxydendrum arboreum

Oriental spruce; see *Picea*

Oxydendrum arboreum
(ok-si-DEN-drum ar-BO-ree-um) **sour-wood, sorrel tree,** Flowers, fruit, fall color, LSP-ESU ○ ◐ ◼◣

Zones: 5 to 9
Height: 30 feet; 75 feet
Foliage: Simple broad-leaved deciduous
Shape: Pyramidal globe, ½ to ⅔ as wide as tall
Characteristics: The sorrel tree, native to the southeastern United States, has one of the longest seasons of interest of any flowering tree. Small white flowers, borne on pendulous stalks, are followed by cream-colored seed capsules that remain showy through summer (making the tree look as if it is still in bloom). In autumn, the seed capsules ripen to brown and remain on the tree for the winter. The foliage is a deep, lustrous green through the summer, turning to yellow and deep red in fall.

Cultural Information: Plant in rich, well-drained, acid soil. Relatively drought tolerant. Minimal pruning is required to remove dead branches.

Pagoda tree, Japanese; see *Sophora*

Paperbark maple; see *Acer*

Parrotia persica (par-ROW-tee-a PER-si-ka) **parrotia,** Flowers, fall color, bark, ESP ○ ◐ ◼◣

Zones: 4 to 8
Height: 20 to 40 feet; 50 feet
Foliage: Simple broad-leaved deciduous
Shape: Spreading globe, sometimes wider than tall
Characteristics: This small tree, native to Iran, often grows with several trunks, but can be trained to a single trunk. It is grown for its bark and brilliant fall color. The bark is of year-'round interest, mottled with gray, green and brown. The lustrous, deep

Parrotia persica

Parrotia persica *(detail of bark)*

green foliage colors to bright orange and yellow in autumn. In early spring, the small flowers with reddish stamens are attractive. Related to witch hazels, winter flowering shrubs.
Cultural Information: Prefers well-drained, acid soil, but will tolerate slightly alkaline soils. Pest and disease free.

Pears, see *Pyrus*

Picea glauca *'Conica'*

Picea pungens *'Glauca'*

Picea (PY-see-a) **spruce,** Evergreen, foliage ○ ◑ ■▪
Zones: Variable
Height: 40 to 60 feet; more than 100 feet
Foliage: Short-needled evergreen
Shape: Pyramidal, ⅓ to ½ as wide as tall
Characteristics: Spruces are among the most common landscape conifers. The most often seen and fastest-growing species is the Norway spruce (*Picea Abies*; Zones 2 to 7, possibly 8; N: Europe). It has dark green needles and a characteristic weeping habit at maturity. While the main branches are held almost horizontally, the smaller branches along them are strongly pendulous, giving the tree an open, airy appearance. This is the most heat-tolerant species and grows to 60 feet or more. White spruce (*P. glauca*) has gray-green foliage and is the most tolerant spruce of wet sites. It is native to northern North America, hardy in Zones 2 to 6 and grows 40 to 50 feet tall. Serbian spruce (*P. Omorika*; Zones 4 to 7; N: southeastern Europe) is one of the finest species and is rapidly becoming popular. It has a very narrow pyramidal shape, requiring less space than any of the others, but may still reach 50 or 60 feet. The needles are deep green with white undersides, which give flashes of white as the branches move in the wind. Grows in both acid and alkaline soils. Another excellent ornamental species is Oriental spruce (*P. orientalis*; Zones 4 to 7; N: Caucasus and Asia Minor). It has shorter needles, a denser habit and is considerably more shade tolerant than the other spruces mentioned here. It also has a slower growth rate, but will eventually achieve 60 feet. *P. o.* 'Aurea' has attractive golden new growth. Colorado spruce (*P. pungens*; Zones 2 to 7; N: Rocky Mountains) is best known in gardens for the grayish blue foliage form of the blue spruce (*P. pungens* 'Glauca'). It has the longest needles and is almost as commonly planted as Norway spruce. It grows to 60 feet.
Cultural Information: Spruces are northern trees and grow best in cool climates. However, they are more successfully grown than firs (*Abies* species) in warm regions (including the Mid-Atlantic states). They prefer a well-drained, moist, acid soil, but are somewhat drought tolerant. *P. orientalis* is susceptible to winter foliage burn in dry, exposed locations. A dense root system makes spruces easy to transplant. Pests and diseases are more serious in southern areas where the trees are stressed by heat. Watch for mites and bagworms in particular.

Pin oak; see ***Quercus***

Pine; see ***Pinus***

Pine, Aleppo; see ***Pinus***

Pine, Austrian; see ***Pinus***

Pine, bishop; see ***Pinus***

Pine, Canary Island; see ***Pinus***

Pine, eastern white; see ***Pinus***

Pine, Himalayan; see ***Pinus***

Pine, Italian stone; see ***Pinus***

Pine, Japanese black; see ***Pinus***

Pine, Japanese umbrella; see ***Sciadopitys***

Pine, Korean; see ***Pinus***

Pine, lacebark; see ***Pinus***

Pine, loblolly; see ***Pinus***

Pine, Scotch; see ***Pinus***

Pine, Swiss stone; see ***Pinus***

Pine, umbrella; see ***Pinus***

Pinus (PY-nus) **pine,** Evergreen foliage, bark, cones ○ ■▪
Zones: Variable
Height: 30 to 60 feet, more than 100 feet
Foliage: Long-needled evergreen
Shape: Pyramidal, about ½ as wide as high
Characteristics: Pines differ from other conifers in their needles, which are held in clusters of twos, threes, or fives. There is remarkable variety in size and adaptation, and many have interesting shapes or variegated foliage. Some become huge trees, whereas others are of slower growth and ideal for small gardens.

The five-needled, or white pines, are especially beautiful due to their bluish or gray-green foliage. In contrast to other pines, they are more northern trees, and do poorly in the South. Eastern white pine (*Pinus Strobus*; Zones 3 to 8; N: eastern North America) is the best known and is frequently used in landscape plantings because of its commercial availability and fast growth. It can become a large tree, exceeding 80 feet (150 feet in the wild), and often outgrows the space provided for it. With age, wet snows snap the brittle branches and leave a picturesque or deformed specimen, depending on your point of view. Long narrow cones hang prominently at the ends of the branches. *P. S.* 'Fastigiata' has upright branches and narrower shape when young, becoming rounded with age. Said to be more resistant to snow and ice damage. Himalayan pine (*P. Wallichiana* or *P. Griffithii*; Zones 5 to 7; N: Himalayan Mountains) is fuller and bushier in appearance owing to its longer needles. A fine ornamental for large properties. The needles of *P. W.* 'Zebrina' are banded with gold. Korean pine (*P. koraiensis*; Zones 3 to 7; N: Korea) has shorter needles and a slower, tighter habit of growth. A refined white pine for smaller properties, it reaches about 40 feet and keeps its low branches. The most refined and shapely white pine is the Swiss stone pine (*P. Cembra*; Zones 4 to 7). It is one of the best pines for small gardens because it is densely branched with a narrow shape, and reaches 40 feet only after many years. Native to mountains of central Europe and southern Asia.

The three-needled pines are more tolerant of heat and have stiffer, sharper needles. Lacebark pine (*P. Bungeana*; Zones 4 to 8), from China, deserves a special situation to show off its beautiful bark, which is mottled with gray, brown and olive green. It is often multitrunked and grows slowly to a height of 30 to 50 feet (75 feet in the wild). Loblolly pine (*P. Taeda*; Zones 6 to 9; N: southeastern United States) is one of the most common pines in the Southeast. It often grows in dense forests, but in open situations it is shorter. It has an open habit and casts a light shade, but requires full sun, even as a young tree. The needles are light green. Canary Island pine (*P. canariensis*; Zones 9 to 10; N: Canary Islands) is an important landscape tree in southern California, with notable long needles. Young trees are conical and pointed in shape, rounding on top as they mature. They usually grow to about 60 feet.

The two-needled pines are a tough and serviceable group. Japanese black pine (*P. Thunbergiana*; Zones 5 to 7; N: Japan and Korea) tolerates coastal salt spray, sandy soils and drought. It is irregular in shape, with a leaning or crooked trunk and seldom grows much above 30 feet. The needles of *P. T.* 'Oculus-draconis' are banded with yellow, giving the tree a beautiful golden cast. Austrian pine (*P. nigra*) is a taller tree, growing 50 to 60 feet (more than 100 feet in the wild). It is characterized by dark green needles, thick branches and a prominent trunk with rough bark mottled gray and brown. It tolerates city conditions, seashore conditions, drought and a range of soils, including those that are high in clay and alkaline. Native to southern Europe, it is hardy in Zones 4 to 7, and possibly 8. Scotch pine (*P. sylvestris*; Zones 2 to 8; N: Europe, northern Asia) has shorter blue-green or yellowish green needles, and orange- or reddish brown bark. It is tolerant of various soils, including poor, dry sites. It normally grows 30 to 60 feet. Aleppo pine (*P. halapensis*; Zones 8 to 10; N: Mediterranean) is useful in California where tolerance of heat, wind, salt and drought are needed. It grows to about 60 feet tall. Bishop pine (*P. muricata*; Zones 7 to 10; N: California) is a finer ornamental than *P. halapensis* and grows to only about 45 feet. Italian stone pine or umbrella pine (*P. pinea*; Zones 9 to 10; N: Mediterranean) is a broad, flat-topped tree that reaches about 80 feet at maturity. The large seeds are the edible pine nuts of Europe. *Cultural Information:* On the whole, pines are better suited to dry, poor soils, hot climates and city conditions than other

Pinus Bungeana *(detail of bark)*

Pinus Wallichiana

conifers. They require good soil drainage. Austrian and Japanese pines are tolerant of salt spray. Austrian pine is susceptible to diplodia tip blight.

Plane tree, London; see *Platanus*

Platanus × acerifolia

(PLAT-a-nus a-sir-e-FO-lee-a) **London plane tree**, Bark, foliage ○ ◐ ▰

Zones: 4 to 8
Height: 70 feet; more than 100 feet
Foliage: Palmately lobed broad-leaved deciduous
Shape: Globe, nearly as wide as tall
Characteristics: The London plane tree originated as a hybrid of the American and Oriental plane trees and proved to be very tolerant of conditions in London and other cities around the world. Unfortunately, it grows too large for cramped spaces along streets and next to buildings, and is losing favor in preference to other smaller city trees now available. As a tree for home landscapes, there are other trees with better habits and more ornamental value. Plane trees drop leaves and twigs all summer, and in autumn shed spherical fruits. The striking bark is mottled with brown, olive and cream, but is shed in large sheets in early summer. There is no significant fall color.
Cultural Information: Grows almost anywhere, including in cities and compacted alkaline soils, which accounts for its popularity for urban planting. Less susceptible to anthracnose than the native sycamore, *Platanus occidentalis*.

Platanus × acerifolia

Plums; see *Prunus*

Poplar; see *Populus*

Poplar, Lombardy; see *Populus*

Poplar, tulip; see *Liriodendron*

Populus (POP-ew-lus) **poplar**,

Foliage ○ ▰
Zones: Variable
Height: 70 feet; 90 feet
Foliage: Simple broad-leaved deciduous
Shape: Fastigiate, globe or pyramidal
Characteristics: Poplars are valued for their fast growth and ability to grow under difficult conditions, including cities and the Midwest. But they are short-lived, weak wooded and subject to a variety of diseases that can seriously disfigure them. Their roots are notorious for growing into and clogging sewer lines and heaving sidewalks and pavement. Many cities prohibit planting them. Poplars must be used with caution in the landscape, and homeowners should resist the temptation of sensational catalog claims. Use them for short-term purposes where trees are needed quickly, but also plant longer-lived, higher-quality trees for the future. Lombardy poplar (*Populus nigra* 'Italica'; Zones 3 to 9) has long been a popular landscape plant for its narrow columnar form, up to 90 feet tall. Unfortunately, it is often seen with dead tops and branches from pest and disease attacks. Originated in the 1600s in the Lombardy section of Italy.
Cultural Information: Grows best in deep, rich, moist soil, either acid or alkaline. Prune in summer and fall, because wounds in winter and spring bleed. Subject to many pests and diseases including many cankers, rusts, mildews, leaf spots, caterpillars, aphids and scales, which can cause serious damage.

Populus nigra *'Italica'*

Port Orford cedar; see *Chamaecyparis*

Portuguese cherry laurel; see *Prunus*

Prunus (PROO-nus) **cherry** and **plum,** Flowers, fall color, bark, SP ○ ◑ ⌙

Zones: Variable

Height: 20 to 50 feet; 70 feet

Foliage: Simple broad-leaved deciduous

Shape: Spreading globe, some weeping, about as wide as high

Characteristics: Flowering cherries and plums are beautiful, small trees with life spans of 20 to 40 years. They mature fast and are perfect for the new homeowner who needs something to grow quickly.

Most are grown primarily for their flowers, but the Amur chokecherry (*Prunus Maackii*; Zones 2 to 6) and *P. serrula* (Zones 5 to 6) are planted for their shiny, smooth or shaggy brownish bark. They dislike summer heat, but are well suited to the north. Both are native to Asia.

Best known among *Prunus* are the Japanese flowering cherries. They have similar landscape use as the crabapples, but they are more graceful in habit, less hardy and lack showy fall fruit. Cultivated in Japan, they are thought to be native to China. *P. serrulata* (Zones 5 to 8) bears the large, double pink-and-white flowers that are usually associated with the Japanese cherries. *P. serrulata* 'Kwanzan' is the cultivar most often planted. It has large, double pink flowers, but is rather stiff in habit compared with other cultivars. Dull red fall color. Higan cherry (*P. subhirtella*; Zones 4 to 8) has more small, deep pink flowers, and blooms a week or two earlier. *P. subhirtella* 'Pendula' is a beautiful weeping cultivar seen in many suburban neighborhoods. *P. subhirtella* 'Autumnalis' has pale pink flowers, some of which open in autumn. *P.* 'Okame' (Zones 5 to 9) is an excellent early flowering hybrid with rich pink flowers. After the petals drop, the red flower stalks remain showy for another few weeks before the leaves emerge. Fall color is orange-red. Yoshina cherry (*P. yedoensis*; Zones 5 to 8) is believed to be a hybrid of *P. serrulata* and *P. subhirtella*. It grows 40 to 50 feet high and is the most floriferous Japanese cherry. The lightly fragrant flowers are pink or white. *P. y.* 'Akebono' ('Daybreak') is a blush pink cultivar of the Yoshina cherry. This cherry makes up most of the planting in the tidal basin in Washington, D.C.

In northern climates, where the large-flowered Japanese cherries are not hardy, the double sweet cherry (*P. avium* 'Plena'; Zones 3 to 7; N: Europe) is a worthy substitute with clusters of large white flowers. Fall color is yellow.

Purple-leaf plum is a striking small tree with deep purple foliage all summer. Most common is *P. cerasifera* 'Thundercloud', hardy in Zones 3 to 8 and native to eastern Europe and western Asia. The light pink flowers are small and not especially showy. *P.* × *blireiana* (Zones 5 to 9) is a hybrid with foliage nearly as purple, and larger double flowers of carmine pink. It is a spectacle when blooming in early spring.

Several evergreen *Prunus* are planted in southern landscapes. Perhaps the most important one is Portuguese cherry laurel (*P. lusitanica*), which has dark green leaves highlighted by reddish petioles (leaf stems) and clusters of white flowers in spring. It grows with one or more trunks, to 20 to 40 feet (the warmer the area, the larger it grows). It is native to Spain and Portugal and is hardy in Zones 7 to 10.

Cultural Information: Plant in well-drained soil, either acid or alkaline, and water in dry spells. Susceptible to many pests and diseases, but these are not normally serious in young, vigorous trees. Older trees should be replaced when they begin to decline. *P. serrula* is especially susceptible to borers. Prune after flowering to remove crossing and undesirable branches.

Prunus serrulata *'Kwanzan'*

Prunus cerasifera

Pseudocydonia sinensis

Pseudolarix Kaempferi

Pseudotsuga Menziesii

Pseudocydonia sinensis (soo-DOH-sy-doh-nee-a sy-NEN-sis) **Chinese quince,** Flowers, fruit, fall color, bark, MSP ○ ◑ ■L▄

Zones: 6 to 8
Height: 20 feet; 40 feet
Foliage: Simple broad-leaved deciduous
Shape: Rounded, not as wide as high
Characteristics: This tree is also called *Cydonia*. The bark—mottled with shades of brown, tan and olive—and the pale pink flowers are this tree's greatest features. In autumn, the foliage changes to yellow and red, and the tree bears large, fragrant, oval, yellow fruit, the size of grapefruits. These fruits are edible (if cooked with a lot of sugar as for jelly), but they may be a nuisance. Don't let one fall on your head! Native to China.
Cultural Information: Grows best in well-drained, acid soil. Susceptible to fire blight. Train to single trunk and prune undesirable and crossing branches to improve shape.

Pseudolarix Kaempferi (soo-doh-LAR-iks KEMP-fer-eye) **golden larch,** Summer foliage, fall color ○ ◑ ■L▄

Zones: 4 to 7
Height: 50 feet; over 100 feet
Foliage: Short-needled deciduous
Shape: Broadly pyramidal, about ⅔ as wide as high
Characteristics: A magnificent deciduous conifer named for its golden yellow fall color. Summer foliage is attractive light green. Also called *Pseudolarix amabilis.* Native to China.
Cultural Information: Prefers a deep, acid, light, well-drained soil. Tolerates air pollution. Pest and disease free.

Pseudotsuga Menziesii (soo-doh-SOO-ga men-ZEE-zee-i) **Douglas fir,** Evergreen foliage ○ ◑ ■L▄

Zones: 4 to 6
Height: 80 feet; more than 200 feet
Foliage: Short-needled evergreen
Shape: Pyramidal, about ¼ as wide as tall
Characteristics: A magnificent conifer, native to western North America. *Pseudotsuga Menziesii* 'Glauca' has blue-green needles and is hardier than those with green foliage.
Cultural Information: Needs a moist, rich, well-drained, acid to neutral soil and prefers climates with high humidity. Subject to wind damage; not suitable for wind breaks.

Purple beech; see *Fagus*

Purple-leaf plum; see *Prunus*

Pyrus Calleryana 'Chanticleer'

Pyrus (PY-rus) **pear,** Flowers, fall color, ESP ○ ◑ ■L▄

Zones: Variable
Height: 20 to 50 feet
Foliage: Simple broad-leaved deciduous
Shape: Pyramidal, globe or weeping, about ⅔ as wide as high
Characteristics: The callery pear (*Pyrus Calleryana*; Zones 5 to 9; N: China) makes a fine ornamental tree with a profusion of white flowers, clean foliage and yellow to red fall color. The fruit is marble size and insignificant. *P. C.* 'Bradford' has been widely planted, but with age, it forms weak branch crotches that split, ultimately disfiguring or destroying the tree. *P. C.* 'Chanticleer' is one of the best alternatives to 'Bradford' callery pears. Grows to 30 feet, or more. Weeping willow-leaved pear (*P. salicifolia* 'Pendula'; Zones 4 to 7; N: southeastern Europe and western Asia) has silvery gray foliage with a weeping habit and grows to about 20 feet.

Pyrus salicifolia *'Pendula'*

Cultural Information: Adaptable to most soils if well drained and not too alkaline. Tolerates city conditions and some drought. Fire blight is a serious problem of pears (especially *P. salicifolia*) in climates with warm summers so they should only be grown in cool climates. Some cultivars of callery pear, such as *P. C.* 'Bradford' and *P. C.* 'Chanticleer' are resistant. Callery pears generally have few pest and disease problems.

Quercus (KWER-kus) oak, Foliage, fall color, evergreen foliage ○ ◑ ▆▖

Zones: Variable
Height: 40 to 80 feet; more than 100 feet
Foliage: Simple or pinnately lobed, broad-leaved, evergreen or deciduous
Shape: Fastigiate to spreading globe, some wider than high
Characteristics: Oaks are strong-wooded, long-lived, quality landscape trees. They are not fast growing and should be planted as part of long-term plans, per-haps in combination with some faster-growing trees. Only deciduous kinds are hardy in the North, but evergreen species are also commonly grown in the South. The acorns provide food for a variety of wildlife.

White oak (*Quercus alba*; Zones 3 to 9; N: eastern North America) must be planted from a container as a small tree, but it is one of the grandest shade trees and can live for hundreds of years. Named for its gray bark. Fall color consists of brownish to reddish tones. Red oak (*Q. rubra*; Zones 4 to 8; N: eastern North America) has blackish bark, deep green leaves and red fall color. Pin oak (*Q. palustris*; Zones 4 to 8; N: eastern United States) is the most commonly planted oak in landscapes because of its compact, easily transplanted root system. It is, however, subject to leaf chlorosis, has poor fall color, and is short-lived. Scarlet oak (*Q. coccinea*; Zones 4 to 9; N: eastern United States) is similar in appearance and more difficult to transplant, but has strikingly beautiful scarlet fall color. Willow oak (*Q. phellos*; Zones 5 to 9; N: eastern United States) is so-called for its smaller, deep green, narrow, willowlike leaves that require less raking. It is a popular landscape tree with a compact, easily transplanted root system. Fastigiate English oak (*Q. robur* 'Fastigiata'; Zones 4 to 8; N: Europe) is narrowly columnar and makes a good substitute for Lombardy poplar. More adaptable to alkaline soil than other oaks.

Evergreen oaks are only hardy in warmer regions. They are long-lived, but grow more slowly and take longer to reach great size than the deciduous oaks. Live oak (*Q. virginiana*; Zones 8 to 10; N: southeastern United States) has deep green leaves and forms a massive rounded tree, broader than high. California live oak (*Q. agrifolia*; Zones 9 to 10) is a useful landscape plant in coastal California. It grows to 80 feet. Canyon live oak (*Q. chrysolepis*; Zones 8 to 10; N: Oregon to southern California) is hardier and smaller, reaching only about 60 feet. The oaks native to the West Coast are adapted to a dry climate and will not survive repeated summer irrigation. Holm or holly oak (*Q. Ilex*) and cork oak (*Q. Suber*) are both evergreens native to southern Europe, hardy in Zones 8 to 10. They grow slowly to 60 feet. Holm oaks are large spreading, densely foliaged trees, good for coastal plantings. The thick bark of cork oak is the source of cork.

Cultural Information: Most oaks prefer a well-drained, acid soil. Pin oak will tolerate wet, poorly drained soils. Scarlet oak and the evergreen oaks from the West Coast and southern Europe are drought tolerant. Some oaks, notably pin oak, will develop chorosis (pale green leaves) when growing in an alkaline soil. Most will grow in shade when young, but all make the best specimens when in full sun. Many are difficult to transplant except as small trees because they have a deep tap root and a far-reaching root system. Willow, pin and red oaks, with short tap roots and fibrous root systems, are easier to transplant. Oaks can be troubled by many pests and diseases, but these are seldom serious.

Quercus alba

Quercus coccinea

Quince, Chinese; see ***Pseudocydonia***

Redbud, eastern; see ***Cercis canadensis***

Red cedars; see ***Juniperus***

Red maple; see ***Acer***

Red oak; see ***Quercus***

Red-vein maple; see ***Acer***

Redwood, coast; see ***Sequoia***

Redwood, dawn; see ***Metasequoia***

Redwood, giant; see ***Sequoiadendron***

Retinospora; see ***Chamaecyparis***

River birch; see ***Betula***

Robinia Pseudoacacia 'Frisia' (row-BIN-ee-a SOO-doh-a-KAY-see-a free-SEE-a) golden black locust, Golden foliage, flowers, LSP ○ ▪️

Robinia Pseudoacacia *'Frisia'*

Zones: 3 to 8
Height: 40 feet
Foliage: Pinnately compound broad-leaved deciduous
Shape: Narrow upright, about ½ as wide as tall
Characteristics: Robinia pseudoacacia 'Frisia' originated in a nursery in Holland and is the only really garden-worthy form of this species (N: eastern United States). It has remarkable canary yellow foliage that maintains its color all summer. The best color will occur in climates with cool summers. Clusters of fragrant white flowers are borne at the ends of the branches. It has an annoying tendency to sprout from the roots all around the tree, often at some distance from the trunk. This is much more of a nuisance in the South than in the North. *R. P.* 'Frisia' is propagated by grafting, and the best-quality trees are grafted low, just above the roots.
Cultural Information: Adaptable to well-drained, acid or alkaline soil. As with other grafted trees, be sure to remove all sprouts from the roots. Stake young trees. Watch for borers and leaf miners. Borer susceptibility decreases when the bark has thickened, after about 10 years.

Salix (SAY-liks) willow, Foliage, fall color, colorful winter twigs ○

Zones: Variable
Height: 30 to 70 feet; 80 to 100 feet
Foliage: Simple broad-leaved deciduous
Shape: Weeping or globe, often as wide as tall
Characteristics: Willows are fast growing and weak wooded. They are also messy when planted along walkways because they tend to drop debris continuously. Willows are the quintessential trees for naturalistic, moist areas. They are so easy to grow that a small branch stuck into moist soil is likely to take root and grow. Golden weeping willow (*Salix alba* 'Tristis' or 'Niobe') is perhaps the most beautiful weeping tree, growing to about 60

Salix alba 'Tristis'

feet. In winter, the golden branches are striking. Other cultivars of *S. alba* are grown for their upright habits and colorful twigs in winter. They should be cut back severely each spring (they grow 6 feet or more annually), to encourage strong, vigorous shoots, which have the best color. *S. a.* 'Britzensis' has red stems, whereas those of *S. a. vitellina* are yellow. *S. alba* is native to Europe and Asia, and is hardy in Zones 3 to 9. The dragon's claw or contorted willow (*S. Matsudana* 'Tortuosa'; Zones 4 to 8; N: China) is a rounded tree to 30 feet with crooked, twisted trunks and branches. Interesting at any season.
Cultural Information: Prefers deep, moist soils, either acid or alkaline. *S. Matsudana* grows in drier locations. Easy to transplant. Susceptible to a variety of pests and diseases, including various cankers, leaf spots, rust, mildew, aphids, caterpillars, scale and borers, but these are not serious problems in healthy, vigorous trees.

Sarvis-tree; see *Amelanchier*

Saucer magnolia; see *Magnolia*

Sawara false cypress; see *Chamaecyparis*

Scarlet oak; see *Quercus*

Sciadopitys verticillata

(sy-a-DOP-it-eez ver-ti-si-LAY-ta) **Japanese umbrella pine,** Evergreen foliage, bark, cones ○ ◑ ▬

Zones: 4 to 8
Height: 15 to 30 feet; 90 feet
Foliage: Long-needled evergreen
Shape: Pyramidal, about ⅔ as wide as tall
Characteristics: A slow-growing conifer with deep green, lustrous, wide needles. The reddish bark is often hidden by the dense foliage. Older trees bear thick-scaled cones, low enough on the tree to be interesting. Japanese umbrella pines are high-quality but expensive ornamentals. They deserve a special location where they can be enjoyed to their fullest. Native to Japan.
Cultural Information: Grows best in rich moist soil. Best with afternoon shade in hot climates. Pest and disease free.

Scotch pine; see *Pinus*

Sequoia sempervirens

(se-KWOI-a sem-per-VY-renz) **coast redwood,** Evergreen foliage, bark ○ ◑ ▬

Zones: 7 to 9
Height: 60 feet; more than 300 feet
Foliage: Short-needled evergreen
Shape: Pyramidal, ⅓ to ½ as wide as tall

Characteristics: Native to coastal California and Oregon, this large conifer has deep green, glossy, flat needles. Reddish bark is attractive in older trees. This species is one of the tallest-growing trees in the world, reaching 370 feet and living for thousands of years. It is much smaller in the short life of a garden. Only the hardiest forms will grow in Zone 7.
Cultural Information: Grow in rich, moist, well-drained, acid soil. Does best where summers are cool and humid as in coastal California and Europe, but is satisfactory, though smaller, in the Southeast.

Sequoiadendron giganteum

(see-kwoy-a-DEN-dron jy-GAN-te-um) **giant redwood, Wellingtonia,** Evergreen foliage, bark ○ ◑ ▬

Zones: 6 to 8
Height: 60 to 100 feet; 275 feet
Foliage: Scalelike needled evergreen
Shape: Pyramidal, ⅓ as wide as tall
Characteristics: A conifer with fine-textured, sharp, scalelike needles, this tree is extraordinary because of its size. It is considered to be the most massive living thing. The reddish bark is curiously thick and spongy. It develops a thicker trunk than the coast redwood, but does not grow as high. The giant redwood may also live for thousands of years. *Sequoiadendron giganteum* 'Hazel Smith' is an especially attractive blue-foliaged cultivar that does well in the East. *S. g.* 'Pendulum' has branches that hang close to the crooked trunk, forming a tall, ghostly-looking tree. Native to California.

Cultural Information: Prefers deep, rich, well-drained soil. Attains the greatest size in western North America and Europe, but grows better than the coast redwood in the East and in areas with low humidity.

Serbian spruce; see *Picea*

Serviceberry; see *Amelanchier*

Service tree; see *Amelanchier*

Shadbush; see *Amelanchier*

Siberian elm; see *Ulmus*

Silk tree, hardy; see *Albizia*

Silver bells; see *Halesia*

Small-leaved linden; see *Tilia*

Snowbells; see *Styrax*

Sciadopitys verticillata

Sequoia sempervirens

Sequoiadendron giganteum

Sophora japonica (so-FOR-ra ja-PON-i-ka) **Japanese pagoda tree,** Flowers, MSU ○ ▬

Zones: 4 to 8
Height: 50 to 70 feet; 70 feet
Foliage: Pinnately compound broad-leaved deciduous
Shape: Globe, about as wide as tall
Characteristics: The pagoda tree, native to China, is valued because it is the last large tree to bloom in summer. The creamy white pea-shaped flowers are followed by green pods that ripen to brown in fall. Leaf color is bright green, but no fall color develops. The tree has a desirable, compact rounded shape. *Sophora japonica* 'Princeton Upright' has a narrower upright habit, good for narrow street locations. *S. j.* 'Regent' is a fast-growing cultivar.
Cultural Information: Adaptable but prefers a light soil, either mildly acid or slightly alkaline. Tends to be susceptible to cold injury in northern areas when young, but settles down after a few years. Tolerant of city conditions. Prune in fall. Needs training as young tree to develop trunk and central leader.

Sorbus Aucuparia

Sorbus (SOR-bus) **mountain ash,** Flowers, fruit, fall color, SP ○ ▬

Zones: Variable
Height: 20 to 50 feet; 60 feet
Foliage: Simple or pinnately compound broad-leaved deciduous
Shape: Rounded pyramidal, about ½ as wide as high
Characteristics: The mountain ashes may have either simple or compound leaves, and white flowers in flat clusters. European mountain ash (*Sorbus Aucuparia*; Zones 3 to 6; N: Europe and Asia) is the species most often planted. The leaves are pinnately compound. It certainly has one of the most striking autumn fruit displays. The berries, borne in large clusters on the ends of branches, are normally orange-red, but cultivars and hybrids are available with pink, yellow and apricot fruit. Fall color varies from greenish yellow to reddish purple, depending on the cultivar and the climate. In undesirable climates, defoliation may occur before fall color develops. *S. Aucuparia* can only be recommended in northern climates with cool summers. It grows 20 to 40 feet. *S. rufoferruginea* 'Longwood Sunset' (Zones 4 to 7; N: Japan) resembles *S. Aucuparia* and has proven to be an excellent ornamental, despite the hot, humid summers at Longwood Gardens, near Philadelphia. It is heat tolerant, has good foliage through the summer, develops burgundy autumn color and bears beautiful crops of orange fruit that persist into late fall. Korean mountain ash (*S. alnifolia*; Zones 3 to 7; N: eastern Asia) looks very different from the familiar mountain

Sophora japonica

Sorbus alnifolia

ashes. It has simple leaves and a broader shape, becoming as broad as high. The flower clusters are smaller but more profuse, and are followed by small reddish fruit, although the fruit is not abundant in warmer climates. Fall color is yellow and orange. Grows 40 to 50 feet.

Cultural Information: Mountain ashes are northern and high-altitude trees; they resent high summer temperatures, which stress the tree and increase susceptibility to pests and diseases. Prevention of pest and disease problems includes watering in dry spells, and mulching to keep the soil cool. The soil should be well drained and acid. Pests and diseases include fire blight, canker, borers, mites, scab, scale and aphids. In stressful situations, trees usually fall prey to canker and borer after a few years.

Sorrel tree; see *Oxydendrum*

Sour gum; see *Nyssa*

Sourwood; see *Oxydendrum*

Southern catalpa; see *Catalpa*

Southern magnolia; see *Magnolia*

Spruces; see *Picea*

Star magnolia; see *Magnolia*

Stewartia (stew-AR-tee-a) **stewartia,** Flowers, fall color, bark, LSP-ESU ○ ◑ ▮▬
Zones: 5 to 7

Height: 20 to 40 feet; 45 to 60 feet
Foliage: Simple broad-leaved deciduous
Shape: Pyramidal, about ½ as wide as tall
Characteristics: The stewartias hold an honored place among small flowering trees. The showy white flowers with golden stamens resemble those of the Franklin tree and camellia. When they fall intact, they carpet the ground with perfectly formed blooms. The bark, mottled with gray, brown and orange, is a yearround feature. Perhaps the Korean stewartia (*S. koreana*) is the most beautiful species, with wide open flowers and yellow and orange fall color. Its small size, to about 20 feet, is ideal for small gardens. The Japanese stewartia (*S. Pseudocamellia*) is very similar but generally grows to 40 feet or more, with more purplish fall color, and cup-shaped flowers.
Cultural Information: Plant in a rich, moist, well-drained, acid soil. Likes to be shaded from hot afternoon sun. A naturally well-shaped tree requiring little pruning, and bothered by few problems.

Stone pines; see *Pinus*

Striped-bark maple; see *Acer*

Styrax (STY-raks) **snowbell,** Flowers, MSP ○ ◑ ▮▬
Zones: 5 to 8
Height: 20 to 30 feet; 50 feet
Foliage: Simple broad-leaved deciduous
Shape: Spreading globe, sometimes wider than high
Characteristics: The snowbells

Stewartia Pseudocamellia

are small, spreading trees with fragrant, nodding, usually white flowers. They are fast growing when young and have clean foliage. Japanese snowbell (*Styrax japonicus*; N: Japan and China) has small leaves and slightly fragrant flowers that hang under the branches. The fragrant snowbell (*S. Obassia*; N: Japan) is a much coarser landscape plant with large leaves and more strongly fragrant flowers in dropping clusters at the ends of the branches.
Cultural Information: Plant in rich, acid, well-drained soil. Not very drought tolerant. Locate in light shade in hot climates. Virtually pest and disease free.

Styrax Obassia

Styrax Obassia (*detail of flower*)

Sugar maple; see *Acer*

Swamp magnolia; see *Magnolia*

Sweet cherry, double; see *Prunus*

Sweet gum; see *Liquidambar*

Swiss stone pine; see *Pinus*

Tatarian maple; see *Acer*

Taxodium distichum

(taks-O-dee-um DIS-tee-kum) **bald cypress,** Foliage, fall color ○ ◑ ◼

Zones: 4 to 9
Height: 70 feet; more than 150 feet
Foliage: Short-needled deciduous
Shape: Narrowly pyramidal, about ¼ as wide as tall
Characteristics: This is the tree of the cypress swamps in the southeastern United States (where it is native). In the wild, they grow in very wet soils where their roots are submerged and the trees often form woody projections from their roots called "cypress knees." In gardens, these knees will form only on old trees planted in wet soil. Bald cypress is similar to dawn redwood, but grows into a narrower, more round-topped tree. With age, it develops more spreading, widely branched crowns. Foliage is soft and feathery, with the short needles arranged along short deciduous twigs. Summer foliage color is light green, becoming rusty orange-brown in fall. A stately and magnificent deciduous conifer.

Cultural Information: Prefers sandy, acid conditions but is adaptable to a wide range of soils—wet, dry, well drained or waterlogged. Young specimens are easy to transplant. Seldom seriously bothered by pests and diseases, although bagworms can be very destructive.

Thread-leaf cypresses; see *Chamaecyparis*

Thuja (THEW-ya) arborvitae,

Evergreen foliage ○ ◑ ◼ ◼
Zones: Variable
Height: 40 to 70 feet; 200 feet
Foliage: Scalelike needled evergreen
Shape: Fastigiate to pyramidal, about ⅓ as wide as tall
Characteristics: Arborvitaes are useful landscape conifers with soft, fanlike foliage. The eastern arborvitae or white cedar (*Thuja occidentalis*; Zones 2 to 8) is native to eastern North America. It is usually a small, narrow tree to 40 feet, and often used for screens and hedges.

Thuja occidentalis *'Emerald'*

Many forms have light green foliage and turn a sickly yellow-green during the winter. These should be avoided in favor of deep green cultivars, such as *T. o.* 'Nigra' and *T. o.* 'Emerald' ('Smaragd'), that hold their color all year long. They also have a tendency to form multiple trunks or double leaders subject to breakage and splitting under snow and ice. Avoid buying multiple-trunked trees. The western arborvitae (*T. plicata*; Zones 5 to 7) is a more massive pyramidal tree from the Pacific Northwest. *T. p.* 'Atrovirens' is an especially fine cultivar that retains its deep green color and makes a shapely specimen. In gardens, it reaches 50 to 70 feet.

Cultural Information: Grows best in rich, moist, well-drained, acid soil, but will tolerate poor drainage. Easily transplanted. Bothered by few pests and diseases, but watch for bagworms and mites, particularly in hot, dry locations.

Taxodium distichum

Tilia cordata (TIL-ee-a kor-DAY-ta) **small-leaved linden,** Summer foliage, fragrant flowers, LSP-ESU ○ ▉▙

Zones: 3 to 7
Height: 60 to 70 feet; 90 feet
Foliage: Simple broad-leaved deciduous
Shape: Pyramidal to globe, about ⅔ as wide as tall
Characteristics: A shapely, medium- to large-size tree with clean, deep green foliage. The yellowish flowers are not showy, but are noticeably fragrant. *Tilia cordata* 'Greenspire' is an especially popular cultivar for its neat, pointed, single-leader habit. Native to Europe.
Cultural Information: An excellent street and city tree that tolerates pollution and a variety of soils. Easily transplanted. Aphids can be a problem because of the honeydew they produce in spring. Japanese beetles can also be a problem.

Tsuga canadensis

Tsuga (SOO-ga) **hemlock,** Evergreen foliage ○ ◑ ● ▉▙

Zones: Variable
Height: 70 feet; 100 to 200 feet
Foliage: Short-needled evergreen
Shape: Pyramidal, about ½ as wide as tall
Characteristics: Hemlocks are widely used landscape plants, particularly useful because they will grow in more shade than any other evergreen conifer. They are widely used for hedges and screening, and as specimen trees. They take clipping very well. Canadian hemlock (*Tsuga canadensis*; Zones 3 to 7) is the most widely used, especially in eastern North America, where it is native. The western hemlock (*T. heterophylla*; Zones 6 to 7) becomes a massive tree to 200 feet in its native habitat along the Pacific coast. It is grown only in the Pacific Northwest where summers are cool.
Cultural Information: Requires a well-drained, moist, acid soil.

Avoid hot, dry, windy locations. Best growth occurs in sun or light shade. Easily transplanted. Many pests and diseases may be found on hemlocks, but the worst are scale and woolly adelgid. They can weaken and kill trees in some areas of the Mid-Atlantic states and New England where they are prevalent. Control them with dormant oil spray.

Tulip poplar; see ***Liriodendron***

Tulip tree; see ***Liriodendron***

Turkish filbert; see ***Corylus Colurna***

Turkish hazel; see ***Corylus Colurna***

Tupelo, black; see ***Nyssa***

Tilia cordata

Ulmus (UL-mus) **elm,** Summer foliage, fall color, bark ○

Zones: Variable
Height: 60 feet; 70 to 80 feet
Foliage: Simple broad-leaved deciduous
Shape: Spreading vase, may become as wide as high
Characteristics: The American elm (*Ulmus americana*; Zones 2 to 9; N: eastern and central North America) was one of our best-loved shade and street trees. Its upright, gracefully vase-shaped, spreading habit, to 80 feet tall, dwarfed everything else and provided high shade. The introduction of Dutch elm disease has killed almost all of them, and they are no longer planted. Research and hybridization with other resistant species is ongoing to find resistant trees with the classical elm shape. *U. a.* 'Liberty' was developed by the Elm Research Institute; it is claimed that this cultivar has high resistance to the disease. The lacebark or Chinese elm (*U. parvifolia*; Zones 4 to 9) is very resistant to the disease and is an excellent ornamental tree. It is usually more spreading than American elm and only grows to about 50 feet. The mottled bark is one of its best features, a mixture of gray, green, brown and orange-brown. Its adaptability and beauty make it an excellent landscape tree. It is native to China, Korea and Japan. The lacebark elm should not be confused with the Siberian elm (*U. pumila*; Zones 4 to 9), which is an inferior, messy and weak-wooded tree.
Cultural Information: Adaptable to wet or dry, acid or alkaline soils. Easily transplanted. The only serious pest is Dutch elm disease, which has effectively eliminated the American elm and several other species from the American landscape. Lacebark elm is highly resistant to the disease.

Ulmus parvifolia

Umbrella pine; see ***Pinus***

Umbrella pine, Japanese; see ***Sciadopitys***

Weeping beech; see ***Fagus***

Weeping nootka false cypress; see ***Chamaecyparis***

Weeping willow, golden; see ***Salix***

Weeping willow-leaved pear; see ***Pyrus***

Wellingtonia; see ***Sequoiadendron***

Western arborvitae; see ***Thuja***

Western hemlock; see ***Tsuga***

Western red cedar; see ***Juniperus***

White ash; see ***Fraxinus***

White cedar; see ***Thuja***

White fir; see ***Abies***

White oak; see ***Quercus***

White pine, eastern; see ***Pinus***

White spruce; see ***Picea***

Willows; see ***Salix***

Willow-leaved pear, weeping; see ***Pyrus***

Willow oak; see ***Quercus***

Winter king hawthorn; see ***Crataegus***

Yellowwood; see *Cladrastis*

Yoshino cherry; see *Prunus*

Zelkova serrata (zel-KOH-va ser-RA-ta) **Japanese zelkova,** Summer foliage, fall color, bark ○ ◐ ◼ ▮
Zones: 5 to 8
Height: 60 to 80 feet; 120 feet
Foliage: Simple broad-leaved deciduous
Shape: Spreading vase, as wide as high
Characteristics: Closely related to the elm, zelkova is becoming increasingly popular as a landscape, street, and shade tree. It is often recommended as a substitute for the American elm, but it does not have quite the same grand, high-arching branches. Although its vase shape is somewhat more stiff, the mottled bark and deep green foliage are very handsome. Fall foliage is yellowish brown to reddish purple. *Zelkova serrata* 'Green Vase' is a tall, fast-growing, upright selection. *Z. s.* 'Village Green' is a hardier, fast-growing cultivar with a more spreading habit and richer red fall color. Native to Japan and Korea.
Cultural Information: Adapted to acid or alkaline soils. Drought and wind resistant when established, but grows best in deep, moist soils. Tolerates city conditions. Highly resistant to Dutch elm disease and other problems that trouble elms.

Zelkova serrata *'Village Green'*

PESTS AND DISEASES

Every landscape is host to pest and disease organisms, but they are usually not serious. Other organisms prey on them and control these problems naturally. This interaction creates a natural balance, something that is important to preserve as much as possible. Resistance of trees to pests and diseases is important in controlling problems naturally, but even resistant trees may become susceptible to attack when they are stressed and weakened by unsuitable conditions. A tree that is not adapted to its location will always have problems. Drought, soil compaction, poor nutrition, pollution, shade in excess of a species's adaptation and hard winters are just a few factors that contribute to poor health. When new diseases or pests are introduced to an area, they can attack trees that have no natural resistance and had previously been free of serious problems. Examples of such introductions are the gypsy moth, Dutch elm disease and the chestnut blight.

It is important to decide when a pest or disease is truly a problem. A few caterpillars can do little damage on their own, and even provide food for wildlife or become beautiful butterflies. A single spot on a leaf is not going to mar the ornamental value of a tree; but when a leaf disease defoliates a whole tree in midsummer, it is a serious problem, at least from the aesthetic standpoint. Take crabapples, for example: Resistant varieties keep their foliage and fruit to maturity with only insignificant infection. Susceptible varieties, however, are often defoliated or their fruit is severely damaged. Even so, the health of the tree may not be seriously harmed, but it can become an eyesore in the landscape. Tulip trees and lindens are susceptible to aphid attacks for a short period in spring when the new foliage is soft. Aphids secrete a sticky substance called honeydew that falls to the ground in tiny droplets, coating surfaces below, and becoming a nuisance on parked cars and patio furniture. The severity of the attack will vary from year to year. Healthy trees don't require control measures because they are not harmed by aphids, but people find them inconvenient. The best solution is not to plant susceptible trees where the honeydew will be a problem. Simply selecting a different species of linden can be a solution, because some kinds are resistant to aphids.

Once the most common shade tree in much of the eastern United States, the American elm, Ulmus americana, *has now been virtually wiped out of the landscape by Dutch elm disease.*

CONTROLLING PESTS AND DISEASES

When a problem starts, take care of it before it gets big. Pick off obvious insects such as caterpillars and bagworms. Wash off aphids and mites with a forceful stream of water—they soon die when deprived of food. Often these measures are enough to prevent an epidemic.

Disease problems can be reduced by avoiding conditions that favor infection, and by sanitation. Most disease spores need wet foliage to germinate and infect plants. Do any watering that will wet foliage early enough for it to dry before nightfall. Good air movement will help dry foliage, and reduce disease generally. Pruning can increase air circulation. Clean up diseased foliage and don't put it in your compost. An infected branch, as in the case of fire blight, should be pruned off before it spreads down into the whole tree.

Chemical pesticides pose problems because they are also toxic to beneficial insects and people. When using them, there is a risk to yourself, your family and friends from the residues. They upset the natural balance of the environment, and can actually perpetuate or create problems by killing the other organisms that work to control your pests. Also, pests and bacteria can build up immunity to chemical controls, making them ineffective and creating a need for stronger chemicals. There are a few environmentally friendly pesticides that are safe for the homeowner to use. Insecticidal soap and horticultural light oil kill only those insects and mites that they touch, with no toxic residue. They are very effective against a wide range of pests, too. Dormant oil sprays are an especially effective way to kill scale insects and eggs of mites; they are sprayed on the trunks and branches when the plants are dormant, and smother the pests by clogging their pores.

Biological pest control methods are becoming more available and are preferred because they are effective without disrupting the natural balance in your garden and in the environment as a whole. The most successful biological control to date is the bacterial disease of caterpillars called *Bacillus thuringiensis* (BT). Caterpillars and some worms are the only organisms that can be infected by this disease. It comes as a powder that you mix with water and spray on the leaves of plants that the caterpillars are eating. It is widely used to control gypsy moths and tent caterpillars. Experience with gypsy moths has shown that BT is the best long-term control. Conventional chemical insecticides also kill the predators of gypsy moth, a situation that perpetuates the epidemic. BT kills only the caterpillars, leaving plenty of predators to carry on the battle against any remaining gypsy moths, and their offspring, in future years. BT can, therefore, be instrumental in creating a balance of predators and hosts.

You can also purchase lady bugs and other predatory insects (usually through the mail) from garden product firms such as Burpee to release in your garden. These controls are less useful for large trees because of the number of predators required. The best overall strategy for controlling pests and diseases is integrated pest management. It simply means that you take a multifaceted approach. Keep your plants healthy and clean. Maintain the natural predator population by not using sprays and poisons indiscriminately. When you encounter a problem, assess whether it is really serious before you act and, when necessary, use the least disruptive control methods. Check the following individual pests and diseases to see which controls are appropriate for your problems.

Ladybug

METHODS OF CONTROL:	9. Remove infected parts; for example, pick off leaves or prune branches.	to break the life cycle of the fungus.
1. Crush pests with fingers or pick off.	10. Maintain sanitary conditions; rake up and dispose of infected leaves.	16. Don't plant the same kind of tree or a related kind in the same place where the infected tree was growing.
2. Wash off with forceful spray of water.	11. Catch pests in traps.	17. Prune out infected branches below signs of disease where wood is unstained; sterilize pruning equipment in 10% solution of chlorine bleach (1 part household bleach to 9 parts water) after each cut.
3. Apply *Bacillus thuringiensis* (Bt) to foliage.	12. Fertilize to increase tree vigor.	
4. Spray with insecticidal soap.	13. Keep foliage as dry as possible; water only early in day so foliage can dry before nightfall.	
5. Spray with light horticultural summer oil.		
6. Spray with dormant oil in early spring.	14. Increase air circulation by thinning surrounding foliage.	18. Spray with neem (Trade name: Margosan).
7. Plant resistant varieties.	15. Eliminate either of the alternate hosts to fungus disease	
8. Poke wires into holes in trunk to kill borers.		

COMMON PESTS OF TREES

APHIDS: Small green, reddish, white, clear or black insects clustered along soft stems and on undersides of leaves that are often distorted and curled. Usually affect trees only in spring. Secrete honeydew in which grows black sooty mold, harmless to the tree but unsightly. Controls: 1, 2, 4, 5 and 18.

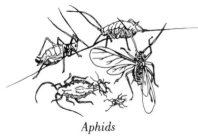

Aphids

MITES: Tiny and difficult to see, they are related to the spider. Often make tiny webs. Leaves become speckled as feed-

Red spider mite

ing destroys chlorophyll, then drop off. Common in hot weather. Controls: 2, 4, 5, and 6.

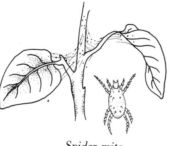

Spider mite

BORERS: Larvae burrow under bark or into trunk and branches. Branches die back. Sawdust evident around holes. Controls: 7, 8 and 9.

LEAF MINERS: Larvae tunnel through leaf, creating visible channels, destroying color and causing defoliation. Controls: 7, 9, 10 and 18.

SCALE: Flat platelike or rounded immobile scales along trunk, branches or on leaves that suck sap and produce honeydew. Crawler stage during

growing season is susceptible to controls 4 and 5 if correctly timed, but control 6 is the standard method. Controls: 1, 4, 5, 6, 9 and 18.

CATERPILLARS: Larvae of moths and butterflies that eat leaves. Not serious in small numbers. Many colors, sizes and markings. Tent caterpillars occur in large groups; they build silk tents in tree crotches for protection. Gypsy moths can defoliate whole trees with their great numbers but are not always serious if predators are active. Sawfly larvae eat needles on pine trees. Controls: 1, 3 and 18.

BAGWORMS: Cocoons hang from ends of branches from which they emerge to feed. They colonize and defoliate conifers, killing the tree. Easy to spot, but often mistaken for cones. Controls: 1, 3 and 18.

JAPANESE BEETLES: Shiny beetles with metallic green sheen eat foliage and flowers of wide

Japanese beetle

range of plants during midsummer. Larvae live in lawns and eat grass roots. Controls: 1, 11 and 18.

MICE AND VOLES: These rodents strip bark and girdle young trees below the snowline or under mulch. Protect with wire or plastic guards specially manufactured for this problem.

RABBITS: Only small trees are in danger from rabbits, which can eat young shoots. They have also been known to strip bark off trunks as high as they can reach when snow covers food supply. Best protection is wire mesh around young plants and around susceptible parts of trunks. Remove or replace wire before it strangles trunk.

DEER: Low branches of trees can be seriously damaged by browsing deer, particularly where deer are overpopulated. Protect by fencing around young trees as high as the deer can reach. Large trees are safe from damage because their branches are out of reach.

Leaves damaged by the following pests, from left; beetles, flea beetles, caterpillars, aphids and leafhoppers.

COMMON TREE DISEASES

ANTHRACNOSE: Particularly serious on sycamore during a wet spring. Trees may be defoliated, but soon grow a new set of foliage. If not defoliated every year, a healthy tree will not be seriously harmed. Controls: 7, 10, 12, 13 and 14.

POWDERY MILDEW: Common on a wide variety of trees and identified by a grayish or whitish coating on the surface of leaves, stems and flower buds. May cause distortion and defoliation. Unless serious, many trees can tolerate moderate infection. Controls: 7, 13 and 14.

CEDAR-APPLE RUST: A fungus disease that alternates in generations between red cedar (juniper) one year and apples, crabapples and hawthorns the next. Cedars develop small round galls among the foliage that produce spores in wet spring weather. A serious infection may cause defoliation on crabapples and hawthorns. Controls: 13, 14 and 15.

FIRE BLIGHT: A bacterial disease that infects crabapples, pears, hawthorns and mountain ashes. Infected branches die back, turning black as if burned. It is spread mostly by bees when pollinating flowers, but also by contaminated pruning equipment. Controls: 7, 9 and 17.

ROOT ROT: Many kinds of fungus can cause root rot in many different trees. Indentification of these requires a specialist. Poor drainage and soil compaction, which weaken a tree, often are contributing factors. Some disease-causing fungi can remain in the soil for many years. Controls: 7 and 16.

SCAB: This fungus infects the fruit and leaves of crabapples, mountain ashes and hawthorns and may cause defoliation. Controls: 7, 10, 13 and 14.

LEAF SPOTS: Many kinds of fungi cause leaf spots on a wide variety of trees. Most trees are only mildly affected and will not be disfigured. Controls: 7, 10, 13 and 14.

DIPLODIA BLIGHT: Die back, beginning with lower branches and working upward on black and Scotch pines. Control: 7.

WILTS: Sudden wilting of a branch or a section of a tree usually indicates the presence of an internal fungus that has cut off sap to the area. Many fungi may cause similar symptoms. Controls: 7 and 16.

DUTCH ELM DISEASE: A serious disease affecting some species of elm, including American elm. Fungus clogs vascular system and inhibits tree's ability to supply water to leaves. Primarily spread by bark beetles. Remove any dead elm trees and infected branches in tree. Controls: 7, 12 and 17.

GARDENERS' MOST-ASKED QUESTIONS

Q: Which flowering trees will bloom in the shade? Which can be used effectively as an understory?
A: Many small flowering trees will grow and bloom well in light shade under tall trees. These include redbuds, dogwood, dove trees, Franklin trees, silver bells, snowbell, stewartias and magnolias. Low branches of large trees that crowd flowering trees beneath should be removed to allow enough light for good bloom.

Q: Which flowering trees make good shade trees?
A: Trees with high spreading branches make the best shade trees. For neatness, they should also drop a minimum of leaves, flowers and fruit through the growing season. Such flowering trees include Japanese pagoda tree, Korean mountain ash and mountain silver bell.

Q: How long does it take for a newly planted flowering tree to flower?
A: This depends on the kind of tree and how it was propagated. Small-growing varieties often flower at a younger age. Most flowering trees are grown from cuttings or by grafting, and usually flower at a younger age than those grown from seed. These trees should flower within two or three years of planting in your yard. Some will flower the first year.

Q: Which trees have the best fall color?
A: Black gums, katsura trees, parrotias and many maples have brilliant red and yellow autumn color. Birches, yellowwoods and ginkgos turn yellow.

Q: Which flowering trees bloom before they produce leaves?

A: Such early flowering trees as Cornelian cherry, flowering dogwood (*Cornus florida*), star and saucer magnolias, callery pear, redbud and many flowering cherries bloom before any leaves have emerged. Crabapples bloom while the leaves are still very small.

Q: Which flowering trees bloom with most tulips? Which with daffodils?
A: The most popular tulips are the Darwin hybrids and the May-flowering varieties such as the single and double lates and lily-flowered types. These bloom along with the redbud, flowering dogwood, horse chestnut and many crabapple varieties. Earlier tulips bloom with daffodils and such trees as saucer magnolia, Japanese flowering cherry and callery pear.

Q: Which bulbs can be planted under flowering trees?

Burpee employees filling orders, 1911.

A: Most spring bulbs need to be planted under deciduous trees, rather than evergreens, so they will receive the early spring sun. Such early blooming bulbs as snowdrops, Siberian squills, and daffodils will grow best. Later-blooming wood hyacinths and camasias will also thrive. They will all last for many years. Tulips usually require more sun and less root competition for best performance and will not last as many years in the garden.

Q: Which flowering trees have four seasons of interest?
A: The following trees are of exceptional interest in the landscape at all four seasons because of a combination of characteristics such as spring or summer flowers, attractive summer foliage, fall color, and fruit, foliage or interesting bark during the winter: crabapple, winter king hawthorn, Chinese quince, Japanese and paperbark maples, sorrel tree, parrotia, mountain ash, stewartia and southern magnolia.

Q: Can I prune flowering trees at any time of the year? Which trees should be pruned when dormant? Which after they bloom?
A: Flowering trees should be pruned only at the proper time or flower buds will be removed, with a decrease in bloom. Spring-flowering trees should be pruned immediately after they flower. Summer-flowering trees can be pruned in the winter or early spring before growth begins.

Q: Do newly planted trees need to be pruned back ⅓ when they are planted:
A: When dormant bareroot trees are planted, new growth will usually be in proportion to the roots, which will begin growing before the top does. Some studies indicate that leaving the terminal buds of the shoots in place actually stimulates faster root growth than when they are removed. Balance the roots and the top by pruning to shape the young tree in other ways, such as removing crowded branches and leaving well-spaced branches with wide crotches, which will form the main trunk and branches. Container-grown trees and balled-and-burlapped trees require even less pruning.

Q: Does pruning improve blooming?
A: When done properly, pruning can improve blooming, but if done incorrectly, it can drastically reduce bloom production. Most trees do not require regular pruning except to correct shape, such as removing crossing branches or preventing narrow crotches from forming. In fact, careless pruning can encourage undesirable suckers and water sprouts. Old trees sometimes form many crowded weak branches that bloom poorly. Thinning these can encourage renewed vigor. Consult a specialized book on pruning for techniques for specific kinds of trees.

Q: Which ornamental trees are the hardiest?
A: Consult the Plant Portraits and The USDA Plant Hardiness Map (page 92) to determine which trees will grow in the coldest climates. Some of the spruces, firs and junipers, as well as eastern arborvitaes, are the hardiest evergreens. The hardiest deciduous trees include maples, larches, crabapples and cherries.

Q: Which trees can be espaliered?
A: Many trees are suitable for training as espaliers, if they are pruned regularly. Those with moderate growth rates are easiest. Some of the easiest to train are crabapples and junipers.

Q: What is the maximum height a tree can be for it to be moved safely? When and how should this be done?
A: The only safe time to move most trees is when they are dormant. Most trees can be moved in the fall, winter or spring, but a few, such as those that are not fully hardy, should be moved only in early spring. If properly done, even very large trees can be successfully moved, but the homeowner is limited by the size of the root ball and soil that can be lifted. Generally, trees under 6 to 8 feet transplant most successfully because they have the vigor to reestablish more rapidly.

Q: Do dogwood really prefer partial shade to full sun? Do they bloom as well in the shade?
A: Dogwood grow best in light shade along the edge of a woods or among tall trees, where they bloom prolifically. Although they will grow in full sun and perhaps bloom even more, they require more water to overcome

the additional heat and drought stress.

Q: *What should I do if I see suckers coming from the ground on my cherry trees? Are they from a different tree? Will they develop into trees themselves? Can they replace the main trunk if it dies?*

A: Many trees, particularly cherries and crabapples, are propagated by grafting onto a different kind of rootstock. The suckers from below the ground are probably coming from this rootstock. They will be inferior to the rest of the tree and may even grow more strongly and crowd out the more desirable top. They will not provide a suitable replacement for the original trunk. The suckers should be cut to the ground as soon as possible, while still small. Fewer suckers will reoccur if they are cut as close to their origin below ground as possible.

Q: *How can I control aphids on my trees when I can't reach the branches to spray them?*

A: Aphids are usually more of a concern and inconvenience to homeowners than they are a threat to the health of their trees. Most trees are only susceptible to large aphid populations in the spring when shoots are young and soft. Aphids soon disappear naturally, without damage to healthy trees. Young trees are most easily damaged by aphids and are also most easily treated by the homeowner. If large trees require control, a professional arborist should be consulted.

Q: *Why are the dogwood in my neighborhood dying? Are the newer types of dogwood (Cornus florida) stronger and more resistant?*

A: In recent years, the flowering dogwood have been attacked by a fungus disease called anthracnose. Several other stresses, such as drought, add to the problem and gradually weaken and kill the trees, branch by branch. There is no single remedy, but keeping your dogwood healthy by fertilizing and watering them in dry spells helps the trees to resist the disease. Also provide good air circulation by planting them in locations where they have plenty of space and trimming away low branches of other nearby trees. The Chinese dogwood is very resistant to anthracnose in most situations. New hybrids between flowering and Chinese dogwood from Rutgers University are also very resistant.

Q: *How can I prevent "lawn mower blight" on my dogwood? Do tree guards work? Do I need them for a mature tree?*

A: Many dogwood, young and old, die from injuries to the base of the trunk that allow entry to disease organisms. The trunk is gradually girdled by this infection, which leads to the death of the tree. Lawn mowers bumping and bruising the bark are the most common cause of such injury. The best solution is to create an area free of grass around the base of the tree, with mulch or a groundcover, to eliminate the need to mow close to the trunk. Enclosing the trunks in tree guards is unsightly and not recommended because it may encourage attacks by borers.

Q: *How can I prevent or treat fire blight on my ornamental pear tree?*

A: Fire blight is most serious in climates with very hot summers. In such climates, it is best not to grow extremely susceptible varieties. Control minor infections by removing blackened infected branches as soon as noticed to prevent the bacteria from moving down the trunk. Prune 12 to 18 inches below any signs of infection and sterilize tools as described on page 81. Avoid heavy fertilization with nitrogen, because the resulting growth is most susceptible to infection. Some varieties of callery pear, such as *Pyrus Calleryana* 'Bradford' are resistant to fire blight.

Please write or call for a free Burpee catalog:

W. Atlee Burpee & Company
300 Park Avenue
Warminster, PA 18974
215-674-9633

APPENDICES

TREES FOR SPECIAL PURPOSES

USUALLY LESS THAN 40 FEET TALL IN LANDSCAPES

Abies koreana
Acer
   A. campestre
   A. ginnala
   A. palmatum
   A. pensylvanicum
   A. rufinerve
   A. tataricum
Albizia Julibrissin
Amelanchier arborea
Carpinus Betulus 'Fastigiata'
Catalpa bignonioides
Cercis canadensis
Chionanthus species
Cladrastis lutea
Cornus species
Crataegus species

Cupressus species
Davidia involucrata
Franklinia Alatamaha
Halesia carolina
Ilex species
Juniperus
   J. chinensis
   J. scopulorum
Koelreuteria paniculata
Laburnum × Watereri
Magnolia species
Malus species
Oxydendrum arboreum
Parrotia persica
Pinus
   P. Bungeana
   P. Cembra

   P. koraiensis
   P. muricata
   P. Thunbergiana
Prunus species
Pseudocydonia sinensis
Pyrus species
Robinia Pseudoacacia 'Frisia'
Sciadopitys verticillata
Sorbus
   S. Aucuparia
   S. rufoferruginea
     'Longwood Sunset'
Stewartia species
Styrax species
Thuja occidentalis

MORE THAN 40 FEET TALL

Abies
   A. concolor
   A. homolepsis
Acer
   A. platanoides
   A. rubrum
   A. saccharum
Aesculus Hippocastanum
Araucaria araucana
Betula
   B. nigra 'Heritage'
   B. platyphylla japonica
     'White Spire'
Calocedrus decurrens
Catalpa speciosa

Cedrus species
Cercidiphyllum japonicum
Chamaecyparis species
Corylus Colurna
Cryptomeria japonica
Cunninghamia lanceolata
× Cupressocyparis Leylandii
Fagus species
Fraxinus species
Ginkgo biloba
Gleditsia triacanthos
Halesia monticola
Idesia polycarpa
Juniperus virginiana
Larix species

Liquidambar Styraciflua
Liriodendron Tulipifera
Magnolia species
Metasequoia glyptostroboides
Nyssa sylvatica
Picea species
Pinus
   P. canariensis
   P. halapensis
   P. nigra
   P. pinea
   P. Strobus
   P. sylvestris
   P. Taeda
   P. Wallichiana

Platanus × acerifolia
Populus species
Pseudolarix Kaempferi
Pseudotsuga Menziesii
Quercus species
Salix species
Sequoia sempervirens
Sequoiadendron giganteum
Sophora japonica
Sorbus alnifolia
Taxodium distichum
Thuja plicata
Tilia cordata
Tsuga species
Ulmus species
Zelkova serrata

WET LOCATIONS

Acer rubrum
Magnolia virginiana
Nyssa sylvatica
Picea glauca
Quercus palustris
Salix species
Taxodium distichum
Thuja occidentalis

TOLERANT OF SUMMER DROUGHT

Calocedrus decurrens
Catalpa species
Cedrus species
Corylus Colurna
Cupressus species
Fraxinus pennsylvanica
Gleditsia triacanthos
Juniperus species
Koelreuteria paniculata
Oxydendrum arboreum
Pinus
  P. canariensis
  P. halapensis
  P. muricata
  P. nigra
  P. pinea
  P. sylvestris
  P. Thunbergiana
Pyrus Calleryana

Quercus
  Q. agrifolia
  Q. chrysolepsis
  Q. coccinea
  Q. Ilex
  Q. Suber
Robinia Pseudoacacia 'Frisia'
Salix Matsudana 'Tortuosa'
Sequoiadendron giganteum
Zelkova serrata

EVERGREEN CONIFERS

Abies
  A. concolor
  A. homolepis
  A. koreana
Araucaria araucana
Calocedrus decurrens
Cedrus species
Chamaecyparis species
Cryptomeria japonica
Cunninghamia lanceolata
× Cupressocyparis Leylandii
Cupressus species
Juniperus species
Picea species
Pinus species
Pseudotsuga Menziesii
Sciadopitys verticillata
Sequoia sempervirens
Sequoiadendron giganteum
Thuja species
Tsuga species

DECIDUOUS CONIFERS

Larix species
Metasequoia glyptostroboides
Pseudolarix Kaempferi
Taxodium distichum

EVERGREEN BROAD-LEAVED

Ilex species
Magnolia grandiflora
Prunus lusitanica
Quercus
  Q. agrifolia

Q. chrysolepsis
Q. Ilex
Q. Suber
Q. virginiana

SPRING FLOWERING

Aesculus Hippocastanum
Amelanchier arborea
Cercis canadensis
Chionanthus species
Cladrastis lutea
Cornus species
Corylus Colurna
Crataegus species
Davidia involucrata
Halesia species
Idesia polycarpa
Laburnum × Watereri
Liriodendron Tulipifera
Magnolia species
Malus species
Parrotia persica
Prunus species
Pseudocydonia sinensis
Pyrus species
Robinia Pseudoacacia 'Frisia'
Sorbus species
Styrax species

SUMMER FLOWERING

Albizia Julibrissin
Catalpa species
Franklinia Alatamaha
Koelreuteria paniculata
Magnolia grandiflora
Oxydendrum arboreum
Sophora japonica
Stewartia species

DECORATIVE FRUIT

Amelanchier arborea
Crataegus viridis 'Winter King'
Idesia polycarpa
Ilex species
Koelreuteria paniculata
Magnolia species
Malus species

Oxydendrum arboreum
Pseudocydonia sinensis
Sorbus species

PARTICULARLY ATTRACTIVE BARK

Acer
  A. griseum
  A. palmatum 'Senkaki'
  A. pensylvanicum
  A. rufinerve
Betula
  B. nigra 'Heritage'
  B. platyphylla japonica 'White Spire'
Cladrastis lutea
Cornus
  C. Kousa
  C. officinalis
Davidia involucrata
Fagus species
Parrotia persica
Pinus
  P. Bungeana
  P. nigra
Platanus × *acerifolia*
Prunus
  P. Maackii
  P. serrula
Pseudocydonia sinensis
Stewartia species
Ulmus parvifolia
Zelkova serrata

TWISTED OR PICTURESQUE BRANCHES

Acer palmatum 'Dissectum'
Fagus sylvatica 'Pendula'
Juniperus chinensis 'Kiazuka'
Salix Matsudana 'Tortuosa'

NARROW, UPRIGHT OR COLUMNAR HABIT

Calocedrus decurrens
Carpinus Betulus 'Fastigiata'
× *Cupressocyparis Leylandii*
Cupressus sempervirens

Ginkgo biloba 'Sentry'
Juniperus
  J. chinensis 'Mountbatten'
  J. scopulorum 'Skyrocket'
Liriodendron Tulipifera 'Fastigiatum'
Magnolia grandiflora 'Hasse'
Picea Omorika
Pinus Strobus 'Fastigiata'
Populus nigra 'Italica'
Quercus robur 'Fastigiata'
Sophora japonica 'Princeton Upright'
Taxodium distichum

WEEPING OR PENDULOUS HABIT

Chamaecyparis nootkatensis 'Pendula'
Fagus sylvatica 'Pendula'
Juniperus scopulorum 'Tolleson's Weeping'
Malus species, some
Prunus subhirtella 'Pendula'
Pyrus salicifolia 'Pendula'
Salix alba tristis
Sequoiadendron giganteum 'Pendulum'

VARIEGATED FOLIAGE

Acer platanoides 'Drummondii'
× *Cupressocyparis Leylandii* 'Silver Dust'
Ilex species, some cultivars
Liriodendron Tulipifera 'Aureomarginatum'
Pinus
  P. Thunbergiana 'Oculusdraconis'
  P. Wallichiana 'Zebrina'

PURPLE FOLIAGE

Acer
  A. palmatum, several cultivars
  A. platanoides 'Crimson King'
Cercis canadensis 'Forest Pansy'

Cryptomeria japonica 'Elegans'
Fagus sylvatica 'Atropunicea'
Gleditsia triacanthos 'Ruby Lace'
Malus species, some
Prunus
  P. × *blireiana*
  P. cerasifera 'Thundercloud'

GOLDEN FOLIAGE

Chamaecyparis
  C. obtusa 'Crippsii'
  C. pisifera 'Filifera Aurea'
Cryptomeria japonica 'Sekkan'
× *Cupressocyparis*
  × *C. Leylandii* 'Castlewellan'
  × *C. Leylandii* 'Robinson's Gold'
Gleditsia triacanthos 'Sunburst'
Picea orientalis 'Aurea'
Pinus Thunbergiana 'Oculusdraconis'
Robinia Pseudoacacia 'Frisia'

BLUE OR GRAYISH FOLIAGE

Abies concolor
Cedrus atlantica 'Glauca'
Chamaecyparis
  C. pisifera 'Boulevard'
  C. pisifera 'Squarrosa'
Cunninghamia lanceolata 'Glauca'
Juniperus
  J. chinensis 'Mountbatten'
  J. scopulorum 'Tolleson's Weeping'
  J. virginiana 'Manhattan Blue'
Picea
  P. glauca
  P. pungens 'Glauca'
Pinus
  P. Cembra
  P. koraiensis
  P. Strobus
  P. Wallichiana
Pseudotsuga Menziesii 'Glauca'
Pyrus salicifolia 'Pendula'

Sequoiadendron giganteum 'Hazel Smith'

TREES FOR SEASHORE

Acer platanoides
Acer rubrum
Aesculus Hippocastanum
Cryptomeria japonica
 ×*Cupressocyparis Leylandii*

Cupressus macrocarpa
Ilex opaca
Juniperus virginiana
Magnolia grandiflora
Nyssa sylvatica
Picea pungens 'Glauca'
Pinus halapensis
Pinus nigra
Pinus sylvestris
Pinus Thunbergiana

Platanus ×*acerifolia*
Quercus agrifolia
Quercus alba
Quercus Ilex
Quercus virginiana
Sophora japonica
Thuja occidentalis
Tilia cordata
Ulmus parviflora

THE USDA PLANT HARDINESS MAP OF THE UNITED STATES

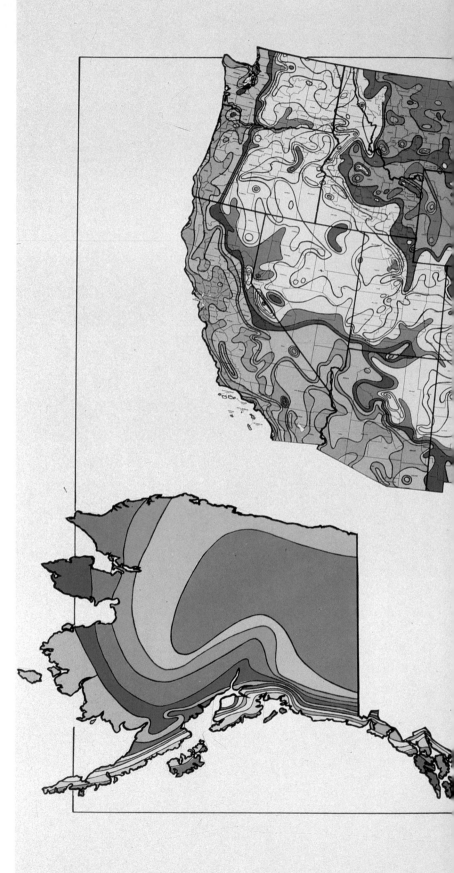

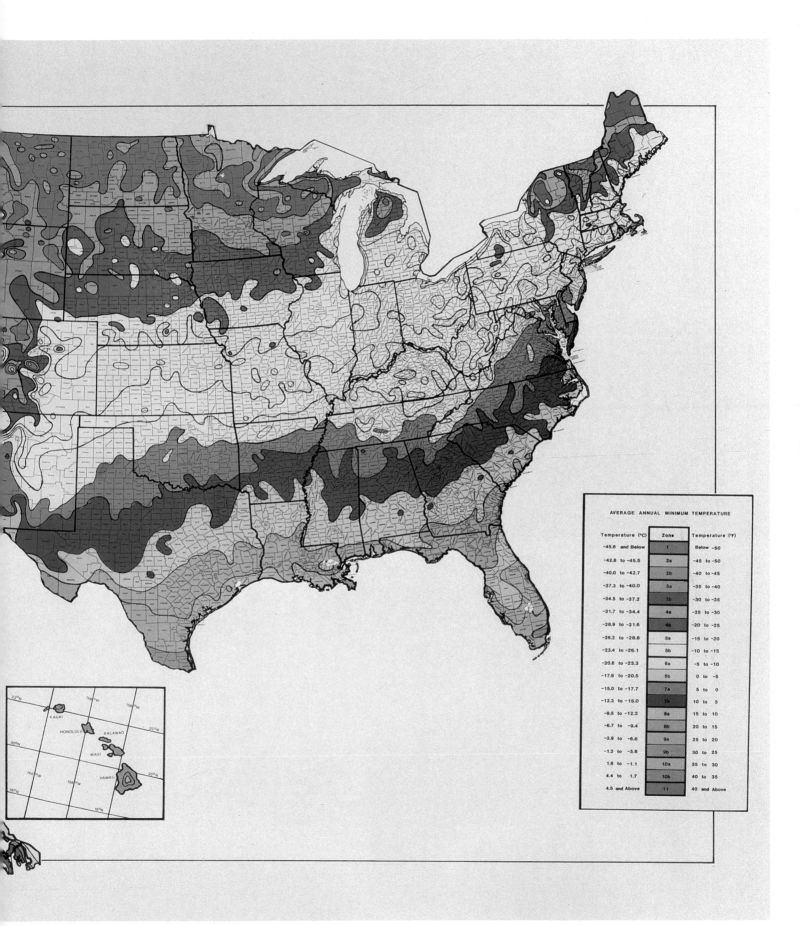

AVERAGE ANNUAL MINIMUM TEMPERATURE

Temperature (°C)	Zone	Temperature (°F)
-45.6 and Below	1	Below -50
-42.8 to -45.5	2a	-45 to -50
-40.0 to -42.7	2b	-40 to -45
-37.3 to -40.0	3a	-35 to -40
-34.5 to -37.2	3b	-30 to -35
-31.7 to -34.4	4a	-25 to -30
-28.9 to -31.6	4b	-20 to -25
-26.2 to -28.8	5a	-15 to -20
-23.4 to -26.1	5b	-10 to -15
-20.6 to -23.3	6a	-5 to -10
-17.8 to -20.5	6b	0 to -5
-15.0 to -17.7	7a	5 to 0
-12.3 to -15.0	7b	10 to 5
-9.5 to -12.2	8a	15 to 10
-6.7 to -9.4	8b	20 to 15
-3.9 to -6.6	9a	25 to 20
-1.2 to -3.8	9b	30 to 25
1.6 to -1.1	10a	35 to 30
4.4 to 1.7	10b	40 to 35
4.5 and Above	11	40 and Above

INDEX

(NOTE: Italized page numbers refer to captions.)